THE SHAMAN'S REVELATIONS
BOOK 5 OF THE SHAMANIC MYSTERIES

Norman W. Wilson PhD

THE SHAMAN'S REVELATIONS
BOOK 5 OF THE SHAMANIC MYSTERIES

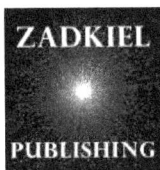

ZADKIEL

PUBLISHING

ISBN: 978-1-78695-210-3

Zadkiel Publishing
An Imprint of Fiction4All
www.fiction4all.com

This Edition
Published 2019

Cover Design:

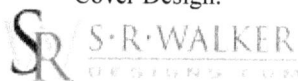

S·R·WALKER

PUBLISHER'S NOTE

FOOTNOTES – references [1] etc are included at the end of the relevant chapter where they occur.

CHAPTER ONE

Know the truth, and the truth shall make you free
John 8:32 (ASV)

"Stop!" Andy yelled.

Budd hit the brakes and his old Ford truck skidded to a halt. Andy opened the door, leaned out of the truck, bent over, and vomited. They relieved their guts these days quite often. Fact was it was a regular occurrence. Andy waited to see if Bud was going next. He wasn't. They'd been that way ever since they worked up at the old Monastery.

Everyone who had worked at The Monastery spoke of it in muted whispers, especially of all the commotion that had gone on up there. A group of crazies was dancing, gyrating in circles. Huge fires were visible. Surely, some of the villagers thought, it was a Dionysian festival. Even as the dozens of workers left the compound, they could smell a peculiar odor about the place; not the musty smell of old, something more rank.

When the action up there really got under way, the villagers thought it was a fireworks' display. But after the second or third explosion, they realized it wasn't. The flashes that burned their way across the night sky were putrid, bile-colored bolts, jagged and sharp. None could remember having seen anything like it. Some thought Mount Baker was erupting. A few of the younger bolder men took it upon themselves to go to the top and find out. They didn't get far. A huge steel gate prevented that. However, in truth, they didn't go that far. The closeness of the lightning strikes turned them back. As the lightening sizzled all around them, they high-tailed it out of there.

"I ain't feelin' so good," Andy said. "Maybe we should turn back. You ain't forgotten what it was like up there?"

"Nope," Budd said as he downshifted gears in the pick-up. "We gotta do something."

The Monastery underwent a massive renovation and even a name change. It was now called Eagles' Crest since a mated pair had honored the site by building a nest in one of the huge trees that stood sentinel-like over the hundred-acre compound. As part of the renovation, the workers cleared some of the trees; drained a deadly methane pond, filled it in, and replaced it with a beautiful fountain, a large bronze eagle with a salmon in its claws. The main entrance to the compound's three-mile-long driveway was a massive gate. Fastened to its steel bars re a sculpted bald eagle and the name Eagle's Crest. At night, those in the little village down at the base of the mountain, could look up at the mountain, and see a gleaming blue-white glow. Despite its name change, the locals still referred to it as The Monastery. It always would be just that for them—The Monastery.

Budd pulled up before the massive steel gate, stopped the truck, rolled down his window, and vomited. He remembered all too well. Even now, however, he didn't realize The Monastery had been the site of a pitched battle—a battle so fierce that the late-night sky exploded with wild bile-green radiation. People in Idaho, Montana, and the southern part of western Canada marveled at the unusual lightning display. He and Andy witnessed the death-throws of the personification of the vilest of evil, the djinni, Moon-Woman.

They stayed late to finish some work in one of the rooms of the main building. When the ferocious clash between the She-Devil and the Healer began, Bud and Andy ran outside and hid in the area where the new fountain stands. Since then they were different, sickly, lethargic, and taken to fits of vomiting. Their skin had turned a yellowish green, and their once dark-brown hair was now snow-white. More than anything, they wanted to look and feel normal.

"Maybe we'll get a financial settlement," Bud said easing his way on out of the pick-up. He pushed a button at the gate's left side. He waited.

The village folks shunned them, unsure of what had happened to them. And like most people, they didn't like change. Understanding the French phrase, plus c'est méme chose was not within their mental processes. Figuring if they got some money, the town's folks wouldn't care if they had a green pallor about them, if they had fits of uncontrolled vomiting, or if the whites of their eyes were yellow.

Bud pushed the gate button again, jabbing his finger hard. "What do you want?" demanded a harsh voice that crackled over a speaker mounted inside a cement column.

"We came to see the Healer. We worked here, and we're sick."

"So what?" snapped the voice.

"We need help," Andy yelled from the cab of the truck.

Several minutes went by. They sat there feeling stupid. "Guess we shouldn't have come up here," Bud said.

The massive steel gate gradually slid open. Bud got back in his truck, started it up, and eased it through once the gate was fully open. Keeping the truck in low gear, Bud slowly drove along the long driveway. Two men with guard-dogs stepped out into the road as they rounded a curve.

"Holy shit! Where'd they come from?" Bud said slamming on the brakes.

"Damned if I know. Better be careful," Andy whispered. He felt sick to his stomach.

"Out!" a giant of a man growled. Jabbing his Uzi at them, he continued, "Put your hands clasped behind your heads and spread your legs."

Too scared not to comply, Bud and Andy spread their legs. The big man's hands searched their bodies. They were sure the big man would crush their testicles. He didn't.

"Okay. Come with me," Samuel ordered. He jabbed his Uzi toward a clump of Daphne shrubs.

They obeyed, sure that they were about to be executed. Instead, he told them to get in the back of an ATV that sat there. The four of them zoomed along the paved road. The guard-dogs raced along behind the ATV. A radiophone squawked.

"Take them to the small conference room and wait there," Paul Dakota said.

Bud nudged Andy as they slid off the back of the ATV. The added huge pillared portico at the front of The Monastery awed them. The place had changed a lot since they had worked here as plasterers. Timidly they followed Samuel up the wide steps. They waited while he punched in a code, turned the handle, and opened the massive doors for them to enter. He escorted them to a small side room halfway down the main corridor.

The room could seat about twenty people. Its shades of blue began dark, lightened as they reached the ceiling, and spread into undulating tints of the base color. Subtle contrasting blue velvet drapes hung on the bank of windows that made up one wall. Posh blue velvet cushioned chairs separated by dark mahogany tables broke the space of the room. Each table had a Tiffany lamp. Their glass shades were also blue. In one corner, sat an 18th-century mahogany secretary. Along another wall, sat a long narrow mahogany table. It held a beautiful set of sterling silver goblets, two decanters, and a pile of neatly folded linen napkins.

"Sit down. Someone will be with you shortly," Samuel said as he left the room.

Andy was sure he heard a click—the sound a door makes when it locked. They both stood there, afraid to sit down. They weren't wearing very clean clothes.

"Oh, Lordy, Lordy! I gotta puke. Can't help it, Bud," Andy said. Frantically, he looked around. He saw no toilet room.

Bud came to his rescue. He handed him a plastic bag. It was something he now took the habit of carrying because he never knew when one or both would need it. Once Andy was done, he dumped his stomach in the same bag. A couple of times, he retched. "Man, I wish I had a beer. My mouth tastes like shit," Bud thought. Instead of sitting down in one of the velvet-covered chairs, he sat down on the marble floor. Andy followed suit. What one did, the other did. They waited, nervously uncertain if the Healer would help them.

CHAPTER TWO

Adam greeted them with a smile, extended his hand to each. They sensed his smile was genuine and that his azure blue eyes held no immediate threat. They'd heard you should watch a man's eyes. That way, you could tell if he was going to get ugly. Since they did not see a threat, they heaved a loud sigh of relief. Adam indicated they should take a seat. He pulled a chair in front of them and sat down. He looked first at Bud and then and Andy searching for any hidden clues as to the reason for their visit. People from the village did not come up to the Monastery. They weren't invited.

"Why didn't you leave the grounds when the rest of the workers did?" Adam said. His voice was so quiet they weren't sure if they heard him.

"How'd you know that?" Bud stammered.

"Yeah. We ain't ever told anybody," Andy said shaking his head to emphasize his comment.

"It would be a good idea if you answered questions rather than asked them," Running-water said. "I'm Paul Dakota, Adam's attorney."

"Where were you hiding?" Adam asked.

"Well, at first we weren't hiding. We had a room to finish up," Bud said.

"Yeah. After that we came out at the back of the Monastery and started around to the front," Andy interrupted.

"And?" Paul said.

"There was a big fire, a really big fire. People going crazy, running around in circles. Drums beating," Bud said.

"Yeah, even the people in town saw it," Andy said.

"Then three guys dressed in fancy Indian costumes and one guy sat down in front of the fire," Bud said.

"He looked just like that guy over there," Andy said pointing at Samuel.

"Uh huh. Then all hell broke loose," Bud said.

"What do you mean by that?" Adam said.

"The sky got real black and then the lightning came, striking everywhere. One bolt nearly got us," Andy said.

"You talk too much," Bud said. The ten and twenty questions annoyed Bud.

"Well ain't what I said true? I tell you, Mr. Adam, the whole place went totally wild. This ugly face appeared in the sky, a woman's face, drooling, and she was screaming at these three Indians. Hundreds of other Indians were running around in circles. Man, it was awesome! Suddenly, the Indian dressed in white doubled up and fell to the ground. That's when things really got hot. You know what I mean. Really hot," Andy said

"Then what?" Paul said.

"These other two Indians turned bright blue and began to vibrate. They vibrated so fast I thought they had disappeared. One of them jumped into this big ball of light. Then, there was a huge flash. I thought the world was ending. You know, Armageddon. The most god-awful scream filled the whole mountain. I have to admit, I pissed my pants right then and there. You did too, Bud. Don't go and lie about it."

"I appreciate your honesty. But what do you want from me?" Adam said.

"Well, ever since that thing happened, we've been different. Our hair is now white, and as you can see, our skin is yellowish green, and the whites of our eyes are yellow. We vomit for no reason. People shun us. Hell, we can't even get laid. Our lives are a mess. We figure you owe us," Bud said.

"How do you figure that? You two were trespassing," Paul said.

"Well, I don't see that we were trespassing. We just didn't get to leave when everyone else did," Bud replied.

"Yeah. That's right. We just got caught in that mess. And that's the God's truth," Andy said.

"Are you asking Adam to pay you?" Paul said.

"I ain't. I want him to help me. I'm sick. Please, Mr. Adam, fix me like I used to be," Andy said.

"And you Bud, what is it, you want?" Adam asked.

"Oh, hell. I'd like to be like I used to be, but I also think you should pay me something for all my misery," Bud replied.

"According to our records, you were paid well above the standard rate for your kind of work. Yet you want more money? I think what you have been paid is more than enough," Paul said.

"I turned my paychecks over to my mother. I gave it all to her, so she wouldn't have to take in laundry anymore. I live on what little I now earn," Andy said.

"I uh banked my money. Put it in an annuity," Bud said.

Adam sensed that Bud was not telling the truth. He recognized that he was the dominant one. It was important that a bond of trust existed between them. That was essential to any healing process he might attempt. Where there's a lie; there's a lack of trust.

"Do you trust me?" Adam asked,

"What ya mean, trust you?" Bud asked.

"You got something in mind?" Andy asked.

"I'm not sure I can do much for you. You have to trust me if I'm to try. Trust is very important. It's the second basis for all that we are," Adam said.

He was sure they didn't understand what he meant by 'trust was the second basis for all that we are.' And he wasn't sure explaining it would benefit the two men in front of him. "You have to trust me, or I can't help you," Adam said.

"I'll do whatever you say," Andy said. He was anxious to get on with it.

"What you plan on doin'? I'd like to know that before I agree," Bud said. He was perspiring.

"Didn't he say we had to trust him? I sure don't know why you came up here if you're going to continue to act like such a dumb ass. What's the matter with you?" Andy grumbled, shaking his head in disgust.

"Okay! Okay. Let's just get it over with," Bud said.

"You have to realize I am not a medical doctor. I do not prescribe medications. I do recommend natural herbs and other ingredients. I am a healer. My hands are healing hands. I detect illness and sometimes the source of that illness. When I do, I then realign the bio-electrodes in the body so that it can heal itself," Adam said. Continuing to explain, "I do that by bringing them into alignment with my own bio-rhythmic pattern."

In the years, they had been together; Paul had never heard Adam explain what it was he did. Not even when he twice saved his own life.

"Look, Adam has saved my life twice," Paul heard himself saying, "once when I had a badly injured kidney and was bleeding to death."

"No kidding. What was the other time?" Andy said.

"When he fought the She-Devil for my soul."

"She-Devil? What the hell's that?" Bud asked.

"That was the face you saw in the sky; a daemonic creature from the Other Side," Paul replied.

"Man, what happened to it?" Andy asked.

"She is no longer. If you want me to try to help you, I suggest we get on with it," Adam said.

"What's that smell in here?" Samuel said as he began to walk across the room.

"The Bag. Gimme the bag," Andy said. Bud pulled the used bag from behind a chair.

"Whew! Give me that," Samuel said. "There's a toilet at the end of the room. Use it. I'll be right back."

"One of you lay down on the floor," Adam said.

Andy went down on his back. He was breathing hard. Adam knelt down beside him, moved his

17

hands just above Andy's outstretched body. At no time did he touch him. Adam's hands didn't turn red; they barely had a blue glow about them. He sensed nothing. Paul watched as Adam knelt beside the outstretched Bud. Nothing. Adam looked up at Paul and sent him a telepathic message.

Weleetka, [1] I can't detect anything. My hands no longer tremble or turn color. I've lost my ability to heal.

The door to the conference room opened. As Esaugetuh strode in Adam stood up.

"Mind if I ask a couple of questions?"

"Of course not, father. You are always welcome," Adam replied.

"Were you near the pond at any time?" Esaugetuh said.

"Well, yeah. We was. We sat there while we ate. Why?" Bud asked.

"You may have a bad case of jaundice. Most likely, the culprit was the methane gas from the pond. A good dose of my karvi torai [2] liquor should clean out the liver," Esaugetuh said.

"Great. I sure could use a drink about now," Bud said.

"Not alcohol. Are you a heavy drinker?" Esaugetuh said.

"No. No, I'm not. We're not. A couple of beers now and then."

"I think they should stay here for a few days. With the karvi, some fresh vegetables, and fruits, I think they'll be just fine," Esaugetuh said. He paused as he took a long look at his son. Adam's life force was weak. "He's dying," Esaugetuh thought. "Got to stop the drain on his system."

[1]   From the Creek language, meaning 'running-water'.
[2] A bitter gourd. Its leaves are placed in a cheese cloth and pounded into a pulp. The cloth is then squeezed to release the juice. The juice is taken internally.

CHAPTER THREE

Once he settled Bud and Andy in one of the rooms on the first floor, Esaugetuh went to his son's office. He didn't bother to knock.

"She left her mark on you didn't she?" Esaugetuh said. He feared Moon-Woman had changed the torus field that surrounded his son's heart. Gently, he touched Adam's face.

"It's strange so very strange. I've tried making a PSI ball and can't. I've tried distant viewing, and I can't. I'm no longer sure if I can always telecommunicate. It is difficult for me to hold my sons. I have no strength to go to my woman. What do you think Old One?" Adam said.

"We need to find what's draining your strength. Come with me outside into the fresh air. Then I'll examine you. I've asked your Dr. Bach to examine our two guests and then come out to look at you. He'll join us when he is free."

Esaugetuh was sure the electromagnetic field surrounding his son's heart had been altered. Adam's lack of color, lack of energy, and the lifelessness of his azure blue eyes was convincing evidence that he was slowly but surely dying. Outside, Esaugetuh had Adam lay down on one of the cedar tables. He passed his hands over his son's body. Unlike Adam's hands, his didn't change color or get hot. Generally, they simply trembled, sending little shock waves up Esaugetuh's arms. There was no trembling. Not even a slight tingle. In an effort to realign Adam's electromagnetic field, Esaugetuh used ground cornflower to make a circle around his son's heart. He then lit a smudge bundle and wafted the sweet-smelling smoke over Adam's body. He walked around him, making sure the smudge had covered him from head to toe. Then he placed his hands around Adam's head, coming from the back of his head, letting his fingers touch the temples. The tingle in his fingers was very weak. Esaugetuh paled. Adam was dying.

Adam eased himself up to a sitting position. His long legs hung over the edge of the table. He closed his eyes, waiting for his father to address him. When he did not, Adam opened his eyes. Esaugetuh was waving at someone in a window on the second floor of the house. When he turned around, Adam saw the troubled look on his father's face.

"What is it, Old One? What have you determined?" Adam said.

Before Esaugetuh could answer, Paul Dakota raced across the manicured lawn.

"What is it, Grandfather? What is wrong?"

"Build a sweat lodge immediately. Get the big man to help you. Have one of the others come and stay with Adam until I return," Esaugetuh said.

"No! I'll stay with Adam. Samuel can put up a pop-up tent. Go get your medicines Old One," Paul said as he pushed a number on his phone. Quickly, he gave instructions to Samuel.

Dr. Back hurried across the lawn to Adam and Paul.

"Take a look at him Doc. What do you think?" Paul said.

Dr. Bach lifted Adam's eyelids, looked into his mouth, and then put his scope to Adam's chest.

"His heartbeat is very slow. Steady but abnormally slow. Probably, I should hospitalize him. Maybe give him an electric shock. That might work for the short term. It will take a number of tests to find out the cause."

Samuel arrived and with a quick twist of his wrist, he had the pop-up open and ready. Inside, Paul dug a fire pit for hot stones. Outside, Paul dug a second fire pit to heat the stones. Paul laid in kindling; placed sticks of hemlock on top of this, and then, using the several bricks left over from the construction, he placed them along the fire pit's edges. Paul lit the kindling. The smell of hemlock soon filled the surrounding area as it caught and took flame. The bricks were not placed directly in the flames because they would crack, break, or explode. He used a shovel to take the heated bricks into the tent. Esaugetuh returned with a large bundle of fresh herbs. He selected them with care. He soaked the whole bundle in a large container of water, laired each across the heated bricks. Soon the little tent filled with sweet-smelling steam. Esaugetuh stuck his head out of the opening and called for Adam to join him. Paul would be the keeper of the fire while Samuel took up his role as guard.

Esaugetuh began to chant. His ancient voice was still mellifluous. Slowly, he danced around his ill son as he beat his inipi drum. The gourd rattles attached to his belt shook in perfect rhythm. He sang his song of healing softly at first, gradually increasing its volume until all could hear it. The tent shook; Esaugetuh did not touch it.

Two women of the household came out. They sat down a distance from the tent. Isha watched her husband. Distress showing on his face matched his nervous pacing. He watched the open flap of the tent. When he saw the steam thinning, he picked up two more heated bricks and took them inside. He added more moistened herbs to the fire pit and then emerged from the tent. The tong-tong drum was singing its praise to the spirits. However, none of those present had drums.

Daphne felt them, vibrantly strong in their pleading voices. She was sure the sounds were coming from the house. Julie didn't play the drums and besides, she was watching the children. Turning to Isha, she said, "I'm going back into the house see who's drumming."

"I'll go. You better stay here in case Adam calls for you," Isha said scrambling to her feet.

"We'll both go. The Old One won't let me in the tent during the healing ceremony. It would break his medicine," Daphne said.

The two women hurried back into the monastery. Hurrying through the large kitchen, down the hallway toward the front of the mansion, to the Great Room, the location of the drumming. It really was a great room, measuring sixty feet in length and fifty feet in width. Lavishly decorated with many authentic Native American art and crafts. It was in this room that the life-sized portrait of Esaugetuh hung above a massive marble fireplace. Among the many Indian artworks were a matched set of drums hanging on one side of the fireplace. These Medicine Eagle drums, designed by artist Cheryl Talking Bird [1], were vibrating; first, one, and then the other in perfect harmony. No one was near them. No one was even in the room. Isha and Daphne turned to go to their children. As Daphne exited, she was sure she caught the glimpse of a shadow. She turned around, looked back into the room. She saw no one. Yet, she sensed that someone was there. She folded her arms across her breasts, hugging herself.

In the living quarters on the second-floor, Daphne found her quadruplets seated in a circle, holding hands, radiating a pale blue light. Their eyes were closed, and they did not respond to their mother's presence. Julie was nowhere to be seen. Nor were Isha's twins. Isha, panic filling her, ran from room to room. Her sons were not there. Rushing back into the sitting room, she found Daphne awed by her sons.

"The twins! I can't find them," Isha said.

"Look on the balcony. The window is open."

Isha found them, with Julie, on the balcony. And like Daphne's quads, they had a blue tone about them and seemed to be vibrating. Their eyes were shut. Julie asleep in a recliner roused herself.

"Oh dear. I must have dozed off. The warm sun. What's that drumming?"

"Esaugetuh is doing a healing ceremony for Adam."

"The twins seem to be in a trance," Julie said.

24

They are fighting for Adam's life," Daphne said. Tears flowed. As hard as she tried, she couldn't stop the sobs that gushed out.

Back in the yard, they waited. Esaugetuh's other two patients emerged and sat down on the grassy lawn, their color already improved. Samuel eyeballed them; they said nothing. The drums in the house continued their harmonious syncopation. The drumming, Esaugetuh's chanting, and dancing continued through the very long night. With the first rays of light's fingers spreading across the sky, all drumming stopped. The chanting stopped. Paul, who continuously renewed the heated bricks during the night, squatted, waiting. With the dawn's arrival, those who waited and watched tensed with mounting anxiety.

"Is he—," Daphne began. Tears spilled out of her blood-red eyes.

"He's still alive. Can't say much more than that. I've done all I can. The She-Devil has left her mark deep in his heart. It has come to me in a vision that he must travel to a sacred place. Weleetka is to go with him. Have your pilot ready the plane. Come with me. Preparations are necessary," Esaugetuh said.

Paul put through a call for Brett. He and Patricia Livingston were just entering the compound. Instead of driving to their cabin, he went to the helipad and began his flight preparations. Patricia Livingston hurried to the Monastery. Paul, busy stashing items into his leather backpack, including his twin Glock 31s, extra ammunition, and cell phone, didn't see her rush by his office. He picked up the house phone and called Dutch Montana, Adam's pilot, and instructed him to bring the jet to Bellingham.

"You done? If you are, I want to put you in a trance so you can see the sacred ground to where you're to take Adam. It's in Arizona, but I am not sure of the exact location. As soon as you know its location, speak out the name," Esaugetuh said.

Paul readily agreed. Unlike Adam when he placed a person under hypnosis, Esaugetuh simply placed a hand on Paul's shoulder and softly spoke to him: "Locate a power site. Zero in on it. Check out its strength. You'll feel its pull. Let it grab you. Get a good picture as to where it is. Remember, once you know, speak out its name."

"A hidden labyrinth in Monument Valley," Paul said.

"Real labyrinth or symbol? Be specific," Esaugetuh urged.

"The Mittens. I see a sign left by the Ancient Ones. It's a symbol carved into the side of a rock, deep within a crevice."

"Where is the crevice located? Which rock?" Exasperated, Esaugetuh had raised his voice, and that broke the hypnotic trance.

"Sorry Old One. I couldn't be more specific," Paul said. Disappointment shot across the lines of his handsome face.

"Hmm. The sun would be setting there now. Which side of The Mittens was the sun?" Esaugetuh asked.

"I think it was at my back, and that means the crevice is to the east of the Mittens."

"You think? Be specific! Was the sun at your back or in your face?"

"My back. It shone down into the crevice revealing the symbol of the labyrinth," Paul said.

"Better. Much better. There is hope. The labyrinth suggests a connection to the source of healing power. You'll need a helicopter and a dune buggy to get to that area. Water and dried jerky will be your food. I will give you medicine to rub on Adam once you're there, and he is in position. It will help attract the power of the place," Esaugetuh said.

"Old One. Come with us. You know much medicine," Paul said.

"I'm too old. I lost much of my own strength in the battle with Moon-Woman. It is better that you go," Esaugetuh replied.

"What if Adam dies? Wouldn't you want to be with him?" Paul said.

"Yes. Of course. I'll go on one condition. If I slow you down you will leave me behind."

"Agreed."

[1] Cheryl Talking Bird is a noted drum painter and maker. She is an enrolled member of the Bois Brule People. She and her husband, Keith, may be reached at the following website:
http://www.earthshadowdesigns.com/theartists.html

CHAPTER FOUR

Samuel helped Paul load Adam into his private helicopter and to secure him in a seat. Once that was done, Esaugetuh boarded. Samuel was to remain behind to protect the women and children.

Within minutes, Brett had the chopper airborne and headed for Bellingham Airport. It was a short flight. The rotor blades barely stopped when Dutch Masters set the Gulfstream V Turbojet down. Once it had come to a halt, the steps were lowered and Will Rexford emerged from the plane. Paul was surprised to see Will. He thought Will was on a new assignment for the government.

Paul and Brett helped Adam get on board the jet. As they did so, Paul detected a different nuance between Dutch, Will, and Brett. Esaugetuh sensed the change also and picked up Paul's concern. Paul called a meeting with the three men before their departure. His primary concern was the arrangements that had been made for them to fly into the Navajo Tribal Park and that the Navajo, as well as the Hopi, had given approval.

"Has the Bell-412 Helicopter been brought into Flagstaff's Pulliam Airport?" Paul asked.

"As far as I know, it has," Dutch Masters replied.

"And has the ATV been loaded and secured?" Paul continued.

"A-okay in that department," Will Rexford chimed in.

"And the other supplies and equipment?" Paul asked.

"Done," Dutch said.

"Okay, Dutch you can check on clearance," Paul said.

He and Will Rexford returned to the cockpit. When Brett got up to join them, Paul stopped him.

"Did you know that Will Rexford would be on board?" Paul said.

"No. I was surprised to see him. Thought he was off in Indonesia? Why?"

"I don't like surprises. I don't see the need for him to be here. You got any idea about the relationship between Dutch and Will?" Paul asked.

"What are you getting at?" Brett said. There was a slight edge in his voice.

"Just wondering. You know how to fly that Bell-412?"

"No. The agency has sent its own pilot and copilot. I don't think even Dutch knows how to fly that one."

"I hear my name mentioned?" Dutch said as he sauntered back into the main cabin. "We expect clearance shortly. By the way, I didn't know the old man was coming."

"And I didn't know Will Rexford was coming. No more surprises, understood?" Paul replied.

"Didn't think it hurt anything," Dutch replied. He was very aware of Paul's tone. "Brett, you coming up front?"

"Once we land at Flagstaff, and we have deplaned, park the jet in hangar number seven. Set security for the plane and you and Will are to remain there. I'm not sure how long we will be gone. I'll notify you when we are ready to return," Paul said.

"No problem. Better get strapped in," Dutch said as he turned to go forward to the pilot's cabin.

Paul made one more check on Adam, made sure Esaugetuh was settled, and then seated himself just outside of Adam's private quarters. As he pulled the seatbelt around him, the memory of an earlier incident at Flagstaff popped into his head. He and Adam were going to an island off the US coast to see the famous reclusive scientist, Dr. Christopher Saint-Michaels. One of Adam's hunches had come all too true, and their plane had been searched before takeoff. A bomb was found in the cockpit. It seemed to him that there had always been someone who wanted Adam dead. He now held everyone suspect. Esaugetuh was not clear of that quiet suspicion that kept growing in his gut. Somewhere, lurking in memories was a statement by Esaugetuh. He had told Adam that there could 'only be one.' "What if he still wants to be the one?" Paul thought. "He was the one with him in the sweat tent. Maybe those herbals—,"

The plane began its taxi down the runway. Within minutes, the Gulfstream Turbojet was airborne and shortly reached its cruising altitude, and leveled off. Paul got up and went to Adam's private quarters. Esaugetuh was seated next to Adam.

"How is he?" Paul asked.

"He's resting. Take a look at this," Esaugetuh said. He pulled back the sheet from Adam, exposing his bare chest.

Over Adam's heart was a dark mark, a miniature claw.

"It's the mark of the She-Devil, Moon-Woman," Esaugetuh said. His voice was barely audible.

"I'll stay with him now. Go and get yourself a brandy. Rest awhile. I'll call you if there is any change," Paul said.

As soon as Esaugetuh had moved forward, Paul leaned over his friend and using telecommunication asked him if he thought he had been poisoned. Adam's eyes fluttered open, took a minute to focus on the distraught face of his soul mate.

"No, Running-water, I've not been poisoned the way you think. Whatever Moon-Woman did, it's creeping through my veins, cancer-like, eating my soul. Remember your promise, my brother. Remember your promise."

"You have my word. I'll take care of your sons and your woman. Put that worry out of your mind. Are you fighting this thing that's eating you?" Paul said.

"I just don't have much strength," Adam said.

"Hmm. Wonder what would happen if you stopped fighting it. Go with the flow, my brother. Your body is fighting with itself. Think of something that brings you a sense of joy," Paul said.

The cabin door opened. Esaugetuh entered. "Running-water is right. Stop fighting. I've

31

prepared an herbal rub for your head. It will help soothe you."

"No!" Paul yelled. He knocked the small dish to the floor. "There will be no rubs, no oils, ointments, or teas. None, you understand?"

Small beads of sweat broke out along his hairline. His breathing quickened. It hadn't been all that long ago that Moon-Woman, pretending to be his grandmother, nearly killed him with her poison tea and foul-smelling liniment. Its terror filled him again, seeing his soul leave his body. Adam grabbed it, held on, and forced it back into his body.

"From now on, no one is to touch Adam but me," Paul thought.

Turning to Esaugetuh, he said," If teas and liniments are to be used Adam will tell me and I will prepare and administer them. I will feed him, rub him down, and bathe him. Whatever it takes, I'll do it. No one is to come near him without my presence. Not even you, Old One," Paul said.

"He is my son, the grown seed of my loins. If what I do brings harm to him, kill me. I will not fight you but listen to what I say. His energy field needs to be replenished. That's why we are going to a place of power. There are certain herbs and plants that help restore one's energy field. Don't deny him that. Nothing, absolutely nothing must be left undone, untried," Esaugetuh said.

"Believe me Old One; I will kill you if necessary. Count on it," Paul said.

And Esaugetuh knew what Running-water said was true. He had survived other such threats over the many years of his life. Admittedly, this one was different. He would put up no resistance. Adam's life was all that mattered to him. "I'm old. My life is complete. Maybe it is a good time to die," Esaugetuh thought.

"So be it," Esaugetuh replied. Then he heard a familiar voice.

Not yet, my father. Not yet. Listen to Running-water. He knows what is in my heart.

Esaugetuh was about to reply. Adam lost consciousness. He replied anyway, "And does he know what is in mine?"

CHAPTER FIVE

The plane touched down at Pulliam Airport. Dutch brought it to a stop in front of hanger number seven. Once everyone had deplaned, he would back it in. He killed the engine and then went back to the main cabin. No one was there. That surprised him. He figured Brett and Will would be there. As he continued on back to the private quarters, he heard a noise coming from one of the plush swivel chairs. It was Will Rexford snoring.

Dutch paused, letting his eyes come to rest upon Will's handsome face. He wondered what he'd look like if he let his hair grow back. When they were kids together, Will had a mop of blond tousled hair that gave him the appearance of having just gotten out of bed. Dutch lingered a bit too long.

"What's up?" Will said.

"We've landed. Just going to check in with Paul."

"Is the chopper ready? We've got Adam on a gurney and ready to move him," Paul said entering the main cabin.

"It should be here. I'll check," Dutch replied.

"I've done that. It's ready to depart as soon as Adam is on board," Brett said joining the group from the plane's office.

"Good. The three of you remain here on the plane. The Old One will go with Adam and me. As soon as we arrive at our destination, I'll call in. Stay alert. Three eight-hour shifts should take care of security," Paul said.

"Why do we have to stay here?" Will Rexford said.

"That's simple. I said so," Paul replied.

"And when did you become chief?" Will grumbled.

Esaugetuh pushed the gurney into the main cabin. Adam struggled to understand what he was hearing. He was sure he had told them to stop their bickering. He tried to raise his head to tell them to knock it off. They seemed light-years away. His eyelids fluttered as he slipped in and out of consciousness unable to determine what was real and what was not. As he laid there waiting, he was sure he heard his father's voice.

"Get out! Get off this plane! Do it now! If you don't I'll blow your damn heads off."

"You gonna shoot me right here. Kill your pilot. Ruin this multi-million dollar jet? Come, old man, you're not fooling anyone. Now put the gun down," Will Rexford said.

"Pilots and planes can be replaced," Esaugetuh said.

That was the last thing Will Rexford heard. His face ripped away by the blast from the double barrel shotgun.

Adam came to, beside himself, he feebly tried to raise his hand. It seemed to him that Paul should have done something. He saw a knife whiz past Paul's head. Dutch Masters staggered.

"You fucking old bastard. Did you really think you could kill me with that little sicker? Think again," Dutch said.

He collapsed on the floor. In his death throes, he realized the knife had been dipped in poison.

A new voice entered Adam's consciousness. "Brett? Yes, it is him. He must have heard the gunfire."

Brett looked down at Adam's face. It was dripping wet. "The chopper's ready any time you are. The ATV and supplies are aboard as you ordered."

Grabbing hold of the gurney, Brett nodded to Paul and began to pull it to the front of the plane. Once on board, Brett helped Paul strap Adam into one of the leather seats. While Paul was seeing to Esaugetuh, Brett, in a single smooth motion, secured the door and gave the pilot a thumbs up. As the Bell-412 began its lift-off Brett said, "I'll give the navigator the coordinates."

It puzzled Paul that Brett's remained on board since he told him to stay with the plane. Yet, he appreciated Brett's efficiency. It was 190 miles to Monument Valley. "Time enough for me to watch him," Paul thought. "Maybe it's nothing; maybe not."

The chief administrator of the Cultural Resource Department of the Navajo Nation graciously granted permission for the chopper to land well within the Monument area and close to The Mittens. The plan was for the helicopter to return to Flagstaff and wait for a call to come back and pick them up. The Bell was posh with her own crew of two. The day was clear, and the heat had not yet begun to build. Brett remained strapped in his seat, quiet, and in no hurry to offer explanations or ask questions. He watched the landscape zoom by. He thought he noticed a slight cough coming from one of the rotors. Dismissed it as imagination.

"Did you notice that little shudder?" Paul asked. "There. Feel that?"

"Yeah. Sure as hell, don't like the sounds of that. Let me check up front."

In the cockpit, the chip indicator was flashing. That meant Ferris metal shavings got into the transmission gearbox. The temperature gauge jumped from green to red. The shimmy became violent vibrations.

"Damn! I got to set this baby down and fast. Hang on," Captain Green said.

"Need any help?" Brett asked leaning into the cabin.

"No. Better buckle up. This is going to be one hell of a ride."

Within minutes, the chopper sat down with a hard thud. The jolt jarred the ATV loose. It shot forward, smashing into the netting across the entrance of the storage area. Like a slingshot, the ATV flew backwards puncturing a large hole in the back of the chopper. Dust from the still rotating blades billowed into the main cabin. Adam's coughing brought Paul and Esaugetuh to their feet. Using a dampened cloth, Esaugetuh bathed his son's face giving moisture to his fever-ridden lips.

"Old One can't you do something? Anything? There must be some ice in the bar. I'll check it," Paul said.

"We need to get him to the sacred ground. Find out how far we are from Tsé Bii Ndzlsgaii," Esaugetuh said.

"The what?" Paul said.

"The Mittens. From there you'll have to take us to the place you saw in your vision. We can't sit here. The heat will finish Adam off."

Paul found the captain on the radio. He was giving coordinates of their crash site. Before turning to Paul, he made sure the directional beacon was functioning. "Everyone okay?"

"Just shook up a bit. Can you tell us far we are from where we were supposed to set down?"

"I'd say we're about six miles out from the touchdown point. I've notified the company, unfortunately, they can't send out another chopper until tomorrow. Everything is out."

"Can't they contact another company?"

"They said they would, but not to count on anything big enough to carry all of us out."

"Damn! Okay, we've got to get the ATV and head out. Time is at a premium," Paul said as he left the cabin.

"Any good news?" Brett asked as he struggled to get out of his seat. He inadvertently hooked his seat belt into the clamp on the adjoining seat.

"No. Doesn't look like any rescue until sometime tomorrow. The Old One and I are going to take the ATV drive Adam out to where we're supposed to be. The pilot thinks we're about six miles out. I want you to stay here. We'll keep in touch with you and let you know when and where to come and get us."

He stepped down from the chopper, turned back to Brett. "Just hope nothing else goes wrong.

Paul could see the outcroppings off in the distance. Their layers of sandstone, siltstone, and shale were beautiful. Their reddish hues created by iron oxide; manganese oxide caused darker streaks of desert varnish.

In his vision, however, they were gold colored and that confused him. Toward their bottoms, the colors looked dark brown. The twin buttes called The Mittens, standing a thousand feet high were stark contrasts for the general flatness of the landscape. For a moment, Paul felt he had been transported to an alien planet. The terrain was rough, filled with Yucca, Bursage, Ratany, and small cacti. Few scrub trees were visible. He spotted an occasional smoke tree. He continued looking out at the vastness that stretched far into the horizon. Wondering what sign he should look for, a sign that would tell him where he was to go. He felt the heat building.

"Not good," he thought. "Got to get a move on."

That broke the hypnotic spell the area had cast over him. Quickly, he loaded the ATV; taking pains to load extra bottled water, blankets, Esaugetuh's bag of medicines, and checked the ten-gallon gasoline cans. He fastened two cans at the rear of the ATV. Because he could not shake a sense of gloom that had taken its hold on him, Paul again checked the two cans of gasoline. He no longer trusted anyone.

Stepping back into the downed chopper, Paul turned and once again looked at the vast emptiness stretching out in front of him. He searched the area, looking for some clue, some sign. A Cactus Wren flew very close to his head; so close that he felt the wind from its rapidly beating wings. It landed in a bush a few feet away. Then he spotted it. For a long moment, he just stared at it. Its orange-red blossoms and sharp-spiny branches screamed recognition at him. It was Adam's Tree! He would never forget that kind of tree. He may have been all of twelve. Back in New Mexico he was playing catch with a couple of his friends and had made a wild dive to catch the ball. He landed in an Adam's Tree. Its thorns tore into his skin. Even now, the memory caused him to wince.

"Hot damn!" Paul said. He had his sign, and it eased some of his doubts about his vision. That small comfort was welcome.

Adam was loaded into the back seat of the ATV. Paul created a tent by using a tarp. He fastened its corners on the back of the seats; it was small protection from the increasing heat. Paul figured they had about six miles to go to get to the first of the Mittens. Then another couple of miles to the second Mitten. Somewhere within that area was a butte with a deep fissure where the labyrinth was painted.

It was going to be rough going. Esaugetuh was a problem. He was old and at times quite feeble. "Man I don't need two invalids," Paul thought.

Sensing Paul's attitude, Esaugetuh hopped into the front seat and waited for him to finish speaking with the crew and Brett. It was an old man's effort to show he was still fit.

Paul revived up the ATV and nearly at the same time felt for his twin Glock-31s. The movement had become so much a part of him, he was sure his guns were married to him. And in one sense, they were. He had vowed never to leave Adam unprotected—a sacred vow made in the name of his spirit guide—a vow he had broken. They were at the ranch in Quebec. He and Adam decided to take a swim in the lake. An unannounced chopper buzzed the ranch, came back, and flew low over the two of them as they scrambled to get to the house. Paul had managed to knock Adam down and jumped on top of him; a futile effort had those on the chopper fired upon them.

Crossing the desert in an ATV with a dying man on board was totally insane; an improbable act, yet here they were, three desert travelers who were not ordinary. Two were shaman, the other bound to both in strange ways. Paul was Adam's soul mate, joined to him in the spirit world, predestined to be his protector. The Old One, Esaugetuh, the Master of Breath, had pumped Adam out of his groin, laid claim to both young men and extracted the highest commitment from each of them. Each would die for the other.

The natural growth and the roughness of the terrain combined with the uncertainty of exact direction forced Paul to travel at a slow speed. He watched for further signs as he drove around bumps, clumps of dried desert grass, small dunes trying to keep the ride as smooth as possible.

Esaugetuh watched in silence. He witnessed much with these two. Paul, Running-water as he preferred to call him, engaged in blazing gun battles to protect Adam: Adam willing to give up a kidney for his friend; fighting the soul-snatcher to save Running-water's soul. Both equally proud to call the other 'brother.' "Much has passed between them," Esaugetuh thought, "but the test they are about to undergo holds a far greater challenge than they know. I'm not sure if I can save either of them. I'm old, and my powers are not as they once were. Fear snaps her hungry jaws at me."

The ATV bumped to a halt, jarring Esaugetuh from his thoughts. Paul hopped off, went to the back, and pulled back the tarp to check on Adam.

Adam's azure blue eyes were dull, fixated in space. Paul passed his hand in front of them; the once lively eyes did not respond. He placed a finger on Adam's carotid artery. He detected no pulse. Panic froze in his throat, choking him. Tears welled up and splashed down along his nose onto Adam's face.

"You trying to drown me?" Adam's voice was barely a whisper.

"Oh! Man! I thought you were dead."

"Not yet. You must let Esaugetuh do his thing, my brother. Remember he is the Master of Breath, and he will give mine back."

"As you wish," Paul said. He gave Adam some water, and wet his face and hands. Then he set the tarp back over Adam, making sure he had plenty of air. He got back onto the ATV, looked around for a sign. He could see the West Mitten standing not too far off, in the distance, a shining red beacon. He headed for it, slowly easing the ATV along a small incline that soon flattened out so he could pick up some speed. Several times, he ran roughshod over low growing scrub plants and narrowly missed hitting a creosote-salt bush, which caused the vehicle to bounce. As they approached, the First Mitten Paul hit a rock, which knocked Adam off his seat onto the floor, lodging him between the back seat and the back of the front seat. Paul turned to see if Adam was all right. The ATV hit a ground squirrel colony's nest. The ATV tipped over spilling passengers and supplies on the ground.

CHAPTER SIX

Immediately, Paul scrambled to his feet; pulled Adam out from beneath the roll bar. Esaugetuh struggled to stand up. Paul caught him as he began to fall. Then he tried to help Esaugetuh to his feet. He cried out in pain.

"I think it's broken," Esaugetuh said.

"Damn! Looks like we've just bought it," Paul said.

"No! Do as I say. Help me set my leg."

"What do I do?" Paul said.

Esaugetuh pushed himself up against the up-ended ATV. "Grab my leg, down by the ankle. When I say pull, yank hard. Really hard. You'll hear a snap. That means the bone has snapped back into place. Then make a splint. You ready?"

"Okay. Just say when."

Esaugetuh reached back of his head, grabbed the front axle with both hands.

"Now!"

Paul yanked the leg. There was a loud snap. Esaugetuh made no sound. Nor did he pass out.

"Jesus. You are one tough old bird, Grandfather."

"That I am. Now then, you need to find something to use to make a splint, and I'll need a crutch. And while you're at it, you better check this front axle. I think it's broken. If it is, you've got a long walk ahead of you. You'll have to carry Adam. Leave me. Now get busy."

The axel was broken. Paul cut several six-inch wide strips from the tarp. Others he made an inch wide. Nothing they had on the ATV would make a splint.

"Cut that cactus; strip it down the sides, cut off the spines. As it dries, it will harden. It'll help heal my leg," Esaugetuh said.

Paul struggled with the cactus. Twice he caught his hands on its razor-sharp needles. Finally, he had most of them scaled off. The skin was tough. By the time he had two usable pieces cut, he was dripping wet from sweat. He placed a section on each side of Esaugetuh's leg, wrapped the six-inch wide canvas strips around those; and then tied that together with the smaller strips.

"Good job. I might make a medicine man out of you yet, even if you are a lawyer," Esaugetuh said.

Despite his pain, the worried look in Esaugetuh's eyes said he knew they were in for a very rough time. He watched Paul tend to Adam, giving him a few drops of water, washing his face and hands. "We'll need one bag of water. There are a couple of leather pouches in my bag of medicines. Fill one with water, and bring the other to me along with the medicine bag itself. I'll choose which herbs I'll want to take with us," Esaugetuh said.

Paul filled one bag with water and took it and the medicine bag to Esaugetuh. He handed him a cup of water. He watched Esaugetuh slowly drink the water, swishing it around in his mouth before swallowing it. "Old One, one bag of water will not be enough."

"You ever drink cactus juice?" Esaugetuh asked.

"Oh, yeah. Once. I was a kid. I shit for a week."

"It'll do that to you if you don't condition yourself to drink it. You need to begin to drink cactus juice. A very little at a time. That way we can save the water for Adam. I can drink the juice. It won't give me the shits." Esaugetuh said.

"Just the same, father of my friend, I'll fill the other pouch with water. I'll bury the remaining containers of water. It'll help protect them from the sun. They'll come in handy on our return trip."

Paul buried the water containers and placed a cairn over them. Paul sat down, exhausted by the exertion and the heat.

"Better wait for a spell. Too hot to travel. Pitch up the rest of that tarp as a cover. Get Adam under it and then use those blankets to make a roof for us. They'll help keep the burning sun off of us. Once it cools down we can move on," Esaugetuh said. Sweat slithered down the crags of his ancient face.

"You doing okay?" Paul asked.

"I'm okay. Find me a crutch."

"I'll look around again a bit later. You want some water?"

"In a bit. In my bag, there's a six-inch piece of hollow plastic tubing. Fish that out and that insert it in a cactus. Pull it back out, blow through one end of the tubing it is clear. Reinsert it into the cactus. You'll also find a small plastic bag in my pouch. Tie that to the end of the tubing. It'll collect the water from the cactus. It'll take about four hours to collect about a cup. I'll drink some of that in order to save the water for Adam. You can drink cactus juice. Not too much. And Running-water, once you have collected the juice, insert a stone in the hole."

Paul noticed Esaugetuh preferred using his Indian name.

"I don't see any need to do that. We'll be on our way and won't have time to collect any more cactus juice," Paul said.

"It will allow the cactus plant to continue to live. Be grateful for that which the earth provides."

"Tell me, Grandfather, how did you learn all this medicine stuff. When did you realize you were a shaman? A hataalii?" Paul asked as he again checked Adam.

"It was my destiny from the day I was conceived. My father was a shaman as was his father before him. I am the seventh of the seventh. My people are an ancient people, and honorable people that populated eastern Canada, Nova Scotia, and what is now the state of Main. Sometimes they migrated into New York and there, mingled with the Mohawk.

My training began very early. I was about four when my father began taking me on long trips into the deep woods. There he would show me each plant and make me learn its shape, taste, and smell. I remember having very little free time. Once he felt comfortable with my plant knowledge, he began animal knowledge. Combined with this was the unmistakable respect for all life forms. One of the few occasions I was given time to play I experienced my first healing. I think I was about twelve. It was a natural thing. One of my friends

47

had fallen on a sharp-pointed stick and was bleeding bad. I placed my hand on the wound, and it's bleeding. Word spread among the tribe that I was a healer. Like all young boys, I had the propensity for showing off. Fortunately, my father, a very wise man, guided me through this stage. I had deliberately wounded a blackbird to show I could heal it. Much to my embarrassment, it died in my hands. I still remember my father's words. He said 'if you deliberately bring pain to a living thing you have violated a trust given you by the Great Spirit. Do not expect to undo the pain you have caused.' The next few years I spent my time learning how to use the various herbs and plants to heal. At age sixteen, I was sent off into the hills for my vision quest." Esaugetuh said.

"Speaking of vision quests, why weren't you available after Adam had his?" It was a blunt question. Lacking the lead-in required for such inquiry. It was the lawyer talking. Paul's face flushed.

"It has saddened me and continues to do so that I was not available to him when he came down from the mountain in Nevada. It was more important that I leave. I had to protect him; not let him know who I really was."

"Protect him? From what?"

"You have already met one from the Other Side, the soul-snatcher, Moon-Woman. She refused goodness and went over. There are others who would destroy those who bring health, well-being to humanity—those who are visionaries. Look what society did to Socrates, Joan of Arc, Gandhi, Martin Luther King, and of course, Jesus Christ."

Esaugetuh's response piqued Paul's instinct for discourse. He realized he had missed that. It would be something he would correct if they survived. "Why? What is there to gain from someone's suffering?"

"Control is exerted by the promise to heal just as there is when a religion promises eternal life if its rules are obeyed. Disobey the rules and you are condemned to eternal suffering. Some healers work that way and demand the surrender of the soul. A good healer will expect payment for his services but not with the surrender of one's soul. Oh, I've known situations when a sick person or the family of the sick person did not pay the healer for his services. The healer retaliated by putting a hex or curse on them," Esaugetuh said.

"Is Adam safe now? I mean besides this current thing."

"I don't know. This illness that attacks his soul is very serious. The She-Devil got her hooks into him before we could stop her. You must prepare for the worst. I know you are willing to die for him, as am I. We may have a chance once we get him to the site of healing power. We have asked so much of the Spirits. It's hard to say if they choose to help us again. Only time will tell. And speaking of time, it is time we got underway. You find me a crutch." Esaugetuh said.

"I better check Adam before we start out. You have something you want me to give him?" Paul said.

49

"Yes. Take two pinches of these herbs and stir them into a small amount of water. Once they are wet, soaked good, rub them on Adam's lips, get a few into his mouth, and rub the rest on his wrists. His skin will absorb it."

"Mind telling me what it is?"

"Creosote Bush. Don't worry. It's not toxic. It acts as a tonic; high in protein and sucrose. And while you're at it, check to see how much cactus juice you've collected. Bring whatever there is to me."

Paul managed to get Adam to swallow a few drops of the tea, put some on Adam's lips and hands. The sun was well behind them now and that meant that had to get moving. Even though they were but a couple of miles from the buttes, the going would be tough. Leaning close to Adam's face, Paul said, "We have to move on as soon as I find a crutch for your father."

Adam struggled to raise his head. "Make a sled out of the tarp. Put me on it; tie it around your waste. Pull me. Don't carry me."

"Of course. Just as you did for Brett coming off the mountain after our crash. Thank you, my brother. The Old One can use me as a crutch if I can't find one for him."

Paul made a wide circle around their make-shift encampment. He felt better. "Hot damn! Adam can still think clearly, and solutions are at hand. Gives a man hope. Hope? It's been written that 'Hope is a lie. That those who hope have nothing else. Hope is a lie to yourself' [1]. Well, for my money, life is hope! Without hope, there is nothing. We hope for a

50

better life, a better job, a better home, for life eternal. And there are some like Adam, who hope for a better world. Out of hope comes inspiration. That brings action—a chance to survive."

Paul decided to right the overturned ATV. It would make it easier to get at some of their gear. With effort, he got Esaugetuh moved a few feet away from the ATV. Next, he moved Adam. He picked out the two extra boxes of bullets; a few packages of beef jerky. He found nothing he could use as a crutch. "Maybe I should just leave him here," he thought.

"I wouldn't do that."

"Adam?"

"Yes. Esaugetuh can read. Watch your thoughts."

Keeping Adam's advice in mind, Paul concentrated on folding the canvas tarp. Once he was satisfied with the fold, he used the duct tape he took from the back of the ATV, taped the side and two ends. In one end, he slit a hole on each side, about eight inches into the canvas. Both of these he taped. Next, he cut the seatbelts out of the ATV, fastened them together, inserted an end into each ole of the canvas, tied them off, and duck-taped them for good measure. The harness and sled were complete. Aware of the rough terrain and that it posed a potential hazard to the canvas sled, Paul emptied two of the plastic water jugs, filled them with sand, and at the opposite end of the sled, he slit two more holes, looped some of the left-over strips from Esaugetuh's leg brace, and tied in a bottle on each side. They made runners on the back end of the sled. Once he was strapped into the harness, it would elevate Adam up enough to prevent the canvas ripping apart.

After some manhandling, Paul secured Adam to the canvas sled. "Time to swallow some more tea. Try to take down a bit more. It's going to be rough going," Paul said. Turning to Esaugetuh he continued, "Found nothing to use as a crutch. You'll have to use me as a crutch. Think you can get up once I'm in the harness?"

"Get down on your knees and bring the harness up under your armpits. I can crawl over to you, lean on you and stand up. Once I'm up, you can stand. Are you sure, you want to do this? Two miles are a long way when you're carrying two invalids," Esaugetuh said.

Paul watched as the old man rolled over on to his belly, and began dragging his leg, using his arms to pull himself along. "Man! He sure is one tough old bird. Jesus, he must feel like Hell has opened up and swallowed him," Paul thought.

"Okay, I'm up. You can stand up now. Remember, get the harness set under your arms. It'll be easier to pull the sled."

Paul eased himself up, slowing reaching his full height of over six feet. He adjusted the harness as he moved his broad shoulders back and forth. He checked his twin Glocks, made sure he had the extra shells, and the single bag of water.

"You got your medicines, Old One? I don't see them on the ground."

"Yes. I'm ready whenever you are," Esaugetuh said wrapping his left arm around Paul's shoulder.

"We stop and rest when you tire. Don't waste your strength."

The three travelers didn't notice the sun's rays playing a symphony of colors along the rocks nor did they hear the bird songs, or notice the few flowering plants. Paul kept his head down. They were still within the ground squirrel colony's digs. The more curious popped their heads up to see who was intruding into their domain. He took one step at a time, stomping down hard before taking the next step. He didn't want to fall through a tunnel, break his own leg, or have Esaugetuh break another one. If the ground felt solid, he took another step. Adam's weight, Esaugetuh hanging on and the effort to move brought torrents of sweat down Paul's back and underarms. The first hour seemed an eternity before it blended into a second. Finally, they were clear of the ground squirrel colony and Paul could increase his pace. The harness, secure at it was, began to eat into his armpits, rubbing the top layer of skin away. The sweat brought severe pain. Esaugetuh noticed.

"Stop! And do it now!"

Grateful for the break, Paul did as he was told. His skin rubbed raw by the straps presented a bloody mess. It took some doing for Esaugetuh to fish around in his medicine bag, hanging on with one arm and standing on one leg. He found what he was looking for.

"I'll need a little water to make a paste. There should be a small cup in my bag. Pour this powder in the cup, add the water, and stir it into a thick paste," Esaugetuh said. "It's ground yarrow. It'll

53

help heal those strap burns. Don't worry it's been around for thousands of years. Lift up your right arm, so I can apply some of this paste. Done. Now the left arm. Let me turn around. Easy now. I don't need my other leg broken."

Once his wounds were dressed, Paul eased Esaugetuh to the ground, so he could check on Adam. He placed a finger on the carotid artery. He waited. Finally, he detected a pulse, slow and steady.

"I should have known," Paul said.

"Known what?" Esaugetuh asked.

"Adam's hypnotized himself to conserve his energy."

"Good. Now cut two four-inch squares from my leather coat. Fold them over, and place them under each strap. They'll help protect your skin. Stop when you need to, and I'll put some more yarrow paste on you. You think you can make the first Butte by nightfall?" Esaugetuh said.

"I don't know. Is it important that we get there by dark?"

"The shale rocks will help keep us warm. The desert gets cold at night. I think we might be in for a storm, and it would be a good idea to have some protection. The winds can get fierce out here in the open. If we can make it there, we'll spend the night. Give you a chance to rest."

"How about you Old One? You doing okay?"

"I'll make it. Help me up."

Paul trudged on. The leather inserts did not ease the pain in his armpits. He had problems keeping the sweat out of his eyes. He felt the desert heat was cooking him alive. The desert hadn't cooled. He caved, not being able to stand it any longer. He stopped; eased Esaugetuh to the ground and plopped down beside him.

"Can you hypnotize me, so I can control the pain and still get us to where we need to go?"

"Yes. But first let me dress those sores once more," Esaugetuh said, as he rummaged around in his medicine bag. "Ah! Got it. This will ease the pain. Stinging Nettles. Close your eyes when I tell you to. I have to blow the Nettle powder under each arm. It'll sting for a few minutes and then you won't feel pain for a couple of hours."

Paul removed his blood-soaked shirt. Seeing this Esaugetuh, with two swift jerks, had his own shirt off and gave it to Paul. "My skin is already weathered and dried up. I don't need a shirt. Put this on and yours will make a good head cover for you."

Leaning over, Esaugetuh took a good long look at Paul and read the pain in his eyes. Close your eyes and raise your arm. I'll tell you when to turn the other to me."

"Damn it all, Old One. You don't have to torture me to death," Paul yelled.

"You'll hear a humming. As soon as you hear it, think of a place that is very pleasant to you. The humming will intensify in pitch."

Esaugetuh snapped his fingers and then gently blew into Paul's eyes. His humming stopped.

"Do you feel any pain?" Esaugetuh asked.

"None."

"When the pain builds just think of the place you pictured in your mind."

"Got it," Paul said as he eased himself back into the harness, remained on his hands and knees until Esaugetuh was standing. He adjusted the harness, slowly stood up, and then headed toward the first Mitten.

The First Mitten is a strange configuration of sandstone and limestone rock towering a thousand feet into the air. The sky, still bright blue, accentuated the Butte's red color' looking at the bottom of the structure, the colors changed to mixed hues of brown-red. Its twin was about two miles east and somewhere beyond that lay the place Paul saw in his vision; the place of the etched picture of a labyrinth.

Like a beacon, Esaugetuh led Paul to the base of the first Mitten. Even though the sun was nearly gone, its afterglow illuminated the Butte in a golden red. They found an area around the Butte that had a slope to it. There under a small ledge, they made camp for the night. Paul, released from his hypnotic state quietly spoke to Adam. Once Adam opened his eyes, Paul again offered some more tea. This time he let it drip slowly into Adam's open mouth. He then laid a cloth soaked in the remaining tea over Adam's face.

Paul tended to Esaugetuh, checking the splint. It had hardened just as Esaugetuh had said it would. "Tell me Old One, is there any swelling? Do you feel feverish? Can you wiggle your toes?"

"I don't sense any swelling, and as you can see I can wiggle my toes. You did a good job with the splint. Drink a very small amount of the cactus juice, and eat a piece of jerky. Chew it very slowly. Give me some and then get some rest."

"Here, take one of these. It's loaded. Just in case. Okay?" Paul said handing him one of his prized Glocks.

That was a first for him. He had never given anybody one of his guns, not even Adam. Somehow, he felt it was the right thing to do. It was an open demonstration of trust. Esaugetuh understood the significance of the gesture and in keeping with his traditional ways, said nothing. They did not build a fire. They counted on the rocks to keep them warm. Exhausted as he was, Paul could not sleep. It wasn't the ground or the raw sores under his armpits that kept him awake. It was dé já vu.

He remembered another time looking up at the beautifully wondrous stars on another clear night. It seemed a long time ago, yet it wasn't. There was a funeral pyre for The Wisdom Keeper at the ranch in Quebec Province. After the ceremony, he and Adam had gone for a walk along the lake and had stopped to talk. The beauty of the night sky fascinated them both. The stars seemed unusually bright. Like here, the night sky was clear and seemingly endless. He thought of counting them but gave up that idea. A Mother Goose rhyme popped into his head. Star light, star bright, First star I see tonight I wish I might have the wish I wish tonight. "Oh man! I must be spooked. I haven't thought of that since I was a kid."

"And what is the wish that you would have?" Esaugetuh's voice broke the silence that surrounded them.

"Ah, mind reading my thoughts are you?"

"Uh uh. And what is your wish?" Esaugetuh repeated.

"I wish that none of us have to die out here, but if it is necessary I wish it to be me."

"Why would you prefer to die if one of us should have to experience that transition?"

"I would not want to live without Adam.

"An interesting answer from two perspectives. One, why would you choose to die and leave a beautiful young wife and two sons? And second, why did you not wish that I should be the one to die?" Esaugetuh said.

"Adam and I are joined. We are soul mates, destined by the Spirits themselves. Our souls are mixed as you well know."

"And why would you not wish that I should die so you both could live?"

"Adam's sons need to know their grandfather."

"That's a weak reason. You never knew your grandfather, and I can't say that it did you any harm."

"Okay, so it's a weak argument. I believe Adam is still going through some kind of transformation. He needs help through that. I can't provide that for him. Only you can."

"So it is agreed then that you should be the one to die," Esaugetuh said.

"Yes."

[1] Dean Koontz. The Darkest Evening of the Year. Bantam Books. New York. 2007

CHAPTER SEVEN

With the sun's rise, Paul was up making a small fire. He would boil some water to make more of Esaugetuh's tea for Adam. Under Esaugetuh's supervision, he made a poultice for himself. Once Adam had had a few drops of tea, Paul applied the poultice to his sore armpits. Its warmth felt good, and he felt it was physically pulling the soreness out. That illusion was short lived. Once he had the harness on, and Esaugetuh standing, Paul began to pull. The pain shot through him with a renewed vengeance. He tried to remember the pleasant place but couldn't bring it into focus. "Take one step at a time. Place o foot in front of the other. Come on! You can do this. Strange a helicopter hasn't been sent out or other search planes. Maybe Brett betrayed us. Maybe he killed the pilot, co-pilot, and was the only one rescued," he thought.

"Stop!" Esaugetuh said.

"What?" Paul replied shocked out of his musings.

"Look at the second Mitten. There it is again. Lightning."

"Good or bad?" Paul said.

"Keep looking and you'll have your answer."

A beautiful rainbow arched its way over the second Mitten. They both wondered if it was a good omen. A jagged bolt of lightning shot through the sky and the rainbow disappeared. Both men accepted signs and searched for their meanings.

"Man, I hope that's a good sign."

"Only time will tell," Esaugetuh said. "Let me put some more Stinging Nettles on your sores. Pull up your shirt. And then have another sip of that cactus juice. Just wet your mouth."

Paul eased Esaugetuh down; making sure his broken leg stretched forward. Once he applied the Nettles to his sores, Paul slipped his shirt back on, and then gave Adam a few more drops of tea. Squatting Indian style, he watched a Gila monster scurry by and then a second. Suddenly, the first turned and lunged at the one that was following it. Fascinated by the battle Paul was unaware of the fast-changing weather.

"Quick. Cover Adam's face. Lay flat on your stomach, cover your head and face with your arms. Leave a small space to breathe. Hurry! Help me roll over. We've got a dust storm coming on fast. Looks like it's gonna be a real Haboob. Most of those thunderclouds we saw earlier, collapsed. My gut feelings tell me this one may last awhile," Esaugetuh shouted.

Paul scrambled. Rolled Adam over, covered him with the tarp sled. Next, he helped Esaugetuh roll over onto his stomach. He untied his bloodied shirt and covered Esaugetuh's head. He hit the ground as the storm rolled in on them, a screaming banshee full of fury.

The wind-driven sand lashed at them, tearing into their clothing, stinging them. Paul struggled to breathe. He felt he was suffocating. He managed to get up on all fours and crawled to Adam. The swirling sand chewed at this face trying to force its way into his mouth and nose.

The wind blew the tarp from Adam. Paul flung himself on top of Adam as a protective shield. The sand quickly piled up around them. He was sure the sand was burying them alive. The sand stung his unprotected hears, cutting small holes in them. Agonizing seconds turned into long painful minutes, and those rolled into a fierce howling hour of relentless torture. The storm stopped. An uncanny stillness hovered over them.

Paul lay there in pain and beaten. Finally sitting up, gasping for air, he shook himself free of the sand. Frantically, he brushed away the sand from Adam, rolled him over.

"You still with me, my brother?"

"I am that I am," Adam whispered.

"Paul you need to move on. Leave me here. Adam has got to get to the healing ground. Once he's settled, you can come back and get me. You can travel much faster if you don't have to be my crutch," Esaugetuh said.

"I don't know why Brett hasn't come looking for us. It seems to me that there should have been a search party out by now. Certainly, Dutch and Will should have been looking for us. Don't you agree?" Paul said.

"No. You told Brett you'd call him when we were ready. He's waiting for that call."

"Shit! I forgot about the two-way. I left it with the ATV. Now what?" Paul was exasperated. Anger swept through him faster than the storm they had just endured. "How could I have been so careless?"

"No time for self-pity. Do as I say. Go without me. Don't worry. I'm tough. Just don't forget where you left me. I figure you got a little over a mile. Now get!"

Paul divided the water, keeping just enough for Adam. He took the remaining cactus juice for himself.

"You still have my gun. Here are some extra shells. As soon as I have Adam settled, I'll come back for you. It may be dark. I'll gather some dried brush so you can build a fire. If I am not back before dark, light the fire. It'll help me find you. Keep a sharp eye, Old One."

"Don't worry about me. I've lived in the desert for many years."

Paul checked on Adam once more and gave him the remaining tea. He then pulled the makeshift harness around his broad shoulders instead of under his arms. The Second Mitten was his beacon, his direction locater, his hope. In spite of the roughness of the terrain, Paul made better time without Esaugetuh attached to his side. The Old One was right. He should have left him behind sooner. As he rounded the base of the Second Mitten still heading east, Paul looked for a sign, any sign that would tell him if he headed in the right direction. He believed in signs. Helios began his evening descent. Searching the horizon for his sign Paul remained still; listening as he looked. Nothing. His heart was racing, and his breathing labored. Desperately, he fought the panic that was taking hold of him.

Then he saw it, a Harris' Hawk. Then a second and third bird followed the first. Hunters all—a family of hunters. He followed their flight and there in front of him was a small raised outcropping; a table. He wondered if it was the same as it had been with Abraham. Was it to be their sacrificial altar? Was it here that he was to lay down his life so that his friend could live?

Stumbling, half running, gasping for breath and still dragging Adam behind him, Paul made it to the outcropping. Quickly, he removed the harness and began his search for the painted labyrinth. He stopped. Idiot! I was looking down at it in the vision. He climbed up on the small Butte, looked around, and then down. There it was.

"Yes!" Paul shouted. "This is it!"

Scrambling back down Paul knocked loose shale, which released a large rock revealing a small natural cave. He didn't take time to find out how big it actually was. He had to get Adam to the top and near the painted labyrinth. Deciding not to attempt dragging the make-ship canvas sled up the side of the table, Paul rolled under Adam, lifted him onto his back, and began the climb. He dug his fingers into the shale, checking its footing before moving on. Inch by agonizing inch he climbed. He heaved himself and Adam over the top and laid there panting. The exertion drained him. He gave Adam a small amount of water, taking a sip of cactus juice for himself. He then tore off a piece of dried jerky, slowly chewed it. Moon-time began its claim on the sky. He had to get moving.

He eased himself back down to the bottom of the Butte. His hands stung from the shale cuts. He stopped, listened, waited. The sound became clearer, closer. Coyote. Damn! Better gather some dried bush for a fire. Adam will need that. Keep them away. He scoured the area around the Butte, finding some sagebrush, dried tumbleweed, and a long stick. He tested it for its strength. He found a cane for Esaugetuh. On his way back to the top, he was sure a coyote snarled. He turned, gun ready. Nothing was there. He busied himself making small fire piles with an easy reach for Adam. He remembered that the number seven was a sacred number and created seven piles of sagebrush, pieces of scrub pine, and dried cactus. Their smell would help cover Adam's smell. Just to make sure that Adam would be safe Paul gave him his other Glock and extra shells and the extra loaded clip.

"You got matches?" Paul said.

"Yes," Adam replied, his voice weak.

"Good. Here are three more. Use them wisely. And you've got the water next to you. Sip a little on the hour."

"Now who's being the mother hen?"

"There are coyotes about. Don't get careless," Paul said.

"You think they smell death, and that's why they are about. Death has not claimed me yet. You better get a move on, my brother. Get my father."

"Okay. Stay alert. I'll be back as fast as I can."

Even with the advance of nightfall, Paul could still see the First Mitten. The moon-glow painted a surreal montage as he trotted along; a lonely figure on the landscape. Once he thought the coyotes were tracking him. He automatically felt for his guns and then remembered he had given them up. He paused, reached down, touched the knife tucked in the top of his boot. Sagebrush blowing in the evening breeze tumbled by him. By the time he had reached Esaugetuh, the moon had arrived at its zenith.

"How is Adam?" Esaugetuh said.

"I have him at the place in my vision. He's waiting for us."

"I see you have found me a crutch. Good. Let me have it. I will use my leather medicine bag as padding. While you rest, let me dress those arms of yours."

Paul chewed a piece of jerky and swished some of the cactus juice around in his mouth. He was surprised that it had not given him the shits. Despite having a crutch, it was still difficult for Esaugetuh to walk. Having been on the ground for so long caused some circulation problems. He dragged the broken leg. A couple of times he nearly fell. For Paul, the pace was agonizingly slow; he held his peace.

"You still got my gun?" Paul asked.

"Yes. Suppose you want it back. It's a nice piece."

"No. Take it out and fire three shots. Wait a space between each shot. Then wait a few more seconds and fire one more. Adam will hear that and know we are getting close."

"Not afraid I'll turn the gun on you?" Esaugetuh said.

"Old One, father of my friend, I figure had you wanted me dead you'd have killed me by now. Fire away."

Esaugetuh pulled the Glock from his waistband, released the safety, and got off three rounds. Waited and on the count of ten fired a fourth shot. He handed the gun back to Paul, who reloaded the gun and tucked into his pants. They heard two rapid shots. Adam heard.

That energized Esaugetuh and he picked up his pace. He now moved with a swing; crutch forward and then he'd swing his leg up to the crutch.

A soft glow in the near horizon from Adam's fire directed them. Once they had reached the table, Paul had to use the tarp to drag Esaugetuh up to the top. Immediately, he checked on Adam and found him remarkably alert and that worried Paul. He knew that all too often just before a person dies, they have a short time of complete alertness, a lucidity that belies their impending death. He wondered for whose benefit such a condition existed. Esaugetuh instructed Paul to make some hot tea and then create some concoction he wanted to be rubbed on Adam's chest, particularly over his heart. Once they had the tea, and Nettle rub, the three of them settled in for the duration of the night.

Night sweats inflamed Adam and frequently he groaned as images of past horrors flooded his mind. The fever returned with intensity. Once he sat up and yelled out a thundering 'no.' Awakened, Paul again applied a tea-soaked compress to Adam's head, wiping his face and hands.

The realization that they were not in control slowly sank into. The sunrise brought that to full fruition with Adam's uncontrollable shaking. Delirium tortured him. Esaugetuh decided that he had to do something else. The herbal tea and herbal rub were not working. "Help me to stand. I will call upon the Spirits. Maybe they will help; maybe they won't."

CHAPTER EIGHT

Standing as straight as he could, Esaugetuh turned his ancient face toward the heavens. He began to pray. The tongue was unfamiliar to Paul.

"Muh-shay-wa-NUH-toe [1]. Great Spirit, I am Esaugetuh, Master of Breath. Hear me."

The sky darkened, and rumblings inched their way to the ears of those on the table Butte. Paul watched in amazement as Esaugetuh grew to a tremendous size. He had seen Adam do that as they fought the terrorists at the ranch in Quebec Province. He didn't have time to wonder how they did this. It would be something he would ask another time.

"And we should be impressed by such a claim?"

Startled that he heard the booming voice, Paul dropped to the ground, guns drawn.

"I am called Phanes [2]. I am of the Cosmic Egg, the source of the universe—the very universe over which you claim dominion. I am the Manifestor. Again, I say to you, hear me. Receive my quest."

"And that is?" The heavens grumbled above them as the booming voice reverberated across the land.

"I ask that our mother, the Earth, and our father, the Sun join to give my son his life. Remove the mark of the She-Devil," Esaugetuh said.

"Make him a bed. Make a paste of the earth upon which you stand. Cover him with it. Then wait. You will be tested."

A bolt of lightning shot across the dark sky. Then silence! Esaugetuh's size was again normal. Paul shook his head trying to clear it. Esaugetuh was standing over Adam, vibrating. He was a conduit of high energy. From his outstretched hands, Esaugetuh passed that energy on to Adam. Adam groaned. The vibrations stopped. The sky cleared changing from dark to a pale yellow and then azure blue. Had Paul taken the time to notice he would have seen that Esaugetuh's eyes matched the color of the sky.

"Did you hear the instructions?" Esaugetuh asked.

"Yes."

Paul opened the tarp, refolded it. Esaugetuh had removed Paul's shirt from his head and handed it to him. "Cut my pants off, take off your clothes, and lay them on the tarp. Get Adam's clothes off and lay them on the tarp. Lay them crossways of one another. Button side facing down."

Esaugetuh scraped up handfuls of the coppery colored dirt; dumped the contents of his leather medicine bag on the ground between his outstretched legs. Then he scooped the dirt into the bag, added the remaining cactus juice, poured in half of their water, and kneaded in some herbs. Carefully, he opened the bag, checked its contents. Satisfied with the consistency of the mixture he said, "Cover Adam with this, from head to toe. And be sure to cover his eyelids."

Paul stripped away Adam's clothes, got him stretched out on the bed of clothing, and began to apply the rub to Adam's face. Adam's nakedness didn't bother Paul. He saw Adam nude many times. Esaugetuh said 'from head to toe.' He hesitated. He had not handled another man's privates before. "So get on with it! He thought."

"Give me your hand," Esaugetuh said as he cut a line across his own palm, letting a drop of blood fall over Adam's heart. Then he cut Paul's hand; held it over Adam's heart to allow the blood to drip.

"There's great power within the earth to heal and there's great power within our bodies to heal. We have given Adam both. Now," he continued using Paul's Indian name, "Running-water, it is up to the power of this sacred place."

He began to chant; something from the old days, dredged up from times past and from past lives. Running-water didn't know the words, but he caught the rhythmic repetitions and added his voice. By its cadence, he knew it was a prayer—a plea for Adam's life. And that was fine with him. Esaugetuh stopped chanting, catching Running-water off guard. Esaugetuh listened.

He heard them before he saw them a nest of rattlers had been disturbed. Neither he nor Running-water was sure if it was their chanting or the warmth of the sun that had brought them out. His skin recoiled as he watched them slither along the warming surface of the shale. An enormous snake, a good sixty inches long, stopped, slithered sideways, coiled and raising its body up nearly half of its length, flicked its tongue tasting the presence of an alien being.

Its broad head moved sideways and then backward and forward as it carefully measured the creature sitting in front of it. Esaugetuh slowly raised his hand, palm outward, drew a circle from left to right. The giant rattler lowered itself a few inches, continuing to taste the air with its tongue.

"What is it, you want, old man?"

"My son is ill and is in need of nourishment. Will you let me have one from your tribe to feed him?" Esaugetuh replied.

"Why should I do that?" The rattler replied.

"Are you less than the great buffalo who gave up members of its tribe so my people could live?" Esaugetuh said.

"The buffalos were stupid. Do you take me for a fool?" The rattler hissed.

"What do you want in return, if you should ask a member of your tribe to give up its life?" Esaugetuh said, keeping his voice quiet and calm.

"Well, it would please me to taste the blood of your young friend and in return, I would give you one of my own to feed your son."

"He has no experience in such things. I will give you my blood," Esaugetuh said as he extended his arm.

The giant rattler reared its huge head in preparation to strike. That was a mistake. Before it could complete its movement, Esaugetuh had its head, clamping its mouth shut. He pulled a knife from his belt and with a single continuous movement, he severed the snake's head.

Turning to the stunned Running-water Esaugetuh said, "You ever skin a snake? If not, this is as good a time as any to learn.

"No, but I'm sure you are about to tell me, right?" Running-water replied.

"You need not concern yourself about poison. The body of the rattler is not poisonous. All its venom is located in sacks inside its mouth. Make a shallow cut beginning at the vent area," Esaugetuh said.

"The vent area? What the hell is that?" Running-water said.

"Its rear end. Cut all the way up, to where the head once was. Then insert a finger under the skin, pull it down until you have it at the tail. Cut the tail and skin off. Roll up the skin. [3] It'll make a nice belt or medicine bag. Cut the meat into chunks to cook over an open fire. You ever ate rattlesnake?"

"No. And I'm not sure I can," Running-water replied.

"It's stringy and chewy. It'll taste like the herbs I'll have you put on it. Roast it over a fire. You'll have to use some of the water to make a broth for Adam. Cut a hunk of the meat into very small pieces and boil. Use our community cup."

By midday, Adam looked like a mummy unearthed from some Egyptian burial site. Every hour on the hour, Running-water gave Adam a few drops of the rattlesnake broth. He double-checked to make sure Adam remained completely covered with Esaugetuh's earth-mixture. That's what he now called it. Concoction just didn't seem right, even though that's how he felt about it.

73

By late afternoon, the sky became a panoramic display of crimson colors intertwined like food coloring in cake batter. Great color swirls floated above the skyline. Running-water was sure they came down from the sky, floated across the Butte and washed over the barely conscious Adam. Esaugetuh lay flat on his back, hugging the warmth of the rocks. Like Running-water, he watched the beauty unfold before them.

"The rattlers may come back to keep warm for the night. Have you got enough fire to keep them at bay? I'm sure they are not pleased that we ate their leader. In the old days, I spread gunpowder around me. They don't like its smell and set up a fierce rattling with their tails. I'd light it and that really put the fear of God into them. I had some shotgun shells in my medicine bag. They must be on the ground here close by."

"The rattlers left for a reason. Must be water close by. I'll go check," Running-water said.

"No! Too dangerous. Ah! Here they are. You know how to open up shells?"

"Yes. What do you want me to do with the powder?"

"Spill the powder around Adam. Use all of it but keep it some distance from him. Give it a tail toward me. And be careful or you'll lose a hand." Esaugetuh warned.

The powder extracted from the shotgun shells was not enough to provide the requested tail to where Esaugetuh sat. Running-water took out two cartridges for the Glock, pried off the tips. He had enough to make the tail. He wondered how they would keep the rattlers from attacking them.

In response to his thoughts, Esaugetuh said, "We'll just have to be careful. I expect they'll come in small numbers to test our defenses. All too often, we underestimate other creations of the Great Spirit. We assume that they lack intelligence. True, they have mastered the art of cunning and wiliness, but we have to be better at it. I will speak to them when they arrive. Maybe some among them will listen."

"That's what you did to their leader? You actually spoke to it?"

"Yes. Cut off this cactus brace. I can't show any sign of weakness. Then help me sit cross-legged, and give me two matches. Hurry."

The hardened cactus splint was difficult to cut through. Finally, it was off and Esaugetuh instructed Running-water to help him stand. He slowly put some weight on his leg. It held. He still needed help to sit back down and get his legs crossed. He fished around in a pocket, pulled out his clay pipe and filled it with red willow bark tobacco, lit it, took a drag, and slowly exhaled its aromatic smell. He used a near-by stick to impale the head of the rattler, which was, then tuck into a small crevice in front of Esaugetuh; a warning to those who would approach.

"You can use my splint to burn. It'll burn fast because it is dry. Cut it into small chunks so it'll last longer. We may be in for a long night."

Scraping announced the arrival of several rattlers. Esaugetuh waited until they were in sight of the small fire Running-water had built. When they saw the head of their former leader, they stopped, coiled, and reared back their heads.

"Ah, so you have come back. My question is this. Have you come to pay homage to the dead tyrant whose severed head you see before you or have you come to praise me for setting you free?" Esaugetuh said.

"You really are a foolish human. Our leader was not a tyrant as you claim. He was our father and we will have our revenge."

"And you have females for your breeding or did your father keep them for himself?"

"Don't change the subject. Of course, we have females," hissed one rattler.

"Ah! And are they young or old crones?" Esaugetuh replied.

Esaugetuh hit a sore point. The two rattlers uncoiled and slithered away. Within a few minutes, three more arrived. These were not interested in talking. While one confronted Esaugetuh, the other two maneuvered to outflank him. A rattlesnake's eyesight is not good; consequently, they did not detect Running-water sitting directly behind Esaugetuh. Even though they depend upon heat sensing, they did not detect two figures. They meet death with swift blows from Running-water's knife. The other one hearing the death throes of his two comrades slithered away.

"You think that's it?" Running-water asked.

"No. They'll come in force this time. You better check Adam before they get here. That last bit of soup you gave him contained an herbal to make him sleep. Can't have him thrashing around.

Running-water knelt beside Adam, leaned over his face, placed his knife close to his mouth. The knife clouded. He was breathing. The paste that he had applied was sun-dried. He paused for a moment and looked at Adam's chest, the spot where he and Esaugetuh had given their blood. There was no movement. He got up and began pacing back and forth, checking and rechecking his guns.

"Stop that damn pacing. Sit down. Be still. Movement attracts them," Esaugetuh grumbled.

Still not content to sit, Running-water lined up several chunks of the cactus splint. Because they were so dry, they would make great firebombs. The light would allow him to see where to shoot. The old warrior and the young one didn't have long to wait. A dozen angry rattlesnakes slithered across the shale.

Running-water tossed a fireball and opened fire as soon as it hit the ground. Unsure of how many he got with the first round, he waited. He heard the movement on the shale.

"One may have slipped by and is headed toward Adam. Now's the time to light that gun powder," Esaugetuh said as he struck a match to the gunpowder tail by his side.

The bright flash from the gunpowder brought Adam upright. Startled, the remaining snakes froze where they were. That momentary pause was all Running-water needed. With rapid fire from both guns, he finished killing the remaining rattlers. Pieces of rock shattered from the rapid firing stung their naked bodies. They waited and listened. A grunt from Adam turned their attention to him.

An Egyptian mummy sat staring at them. The image brought peals of laughter from Esaugetuh and Running-water. As Adam moved, the dried past cracked and began to tumble away.

"I wouldn't laugh if I were you. Looks who's in their underwear?"

"Yeah. Well at least we aren't naked," Running-water said between fits of raucous laughter.

And the three of them laughed together. It was a laughter filled with the nervous knowledge that they had survived once again; the kind that says you're damn grateful.

"What in tarnation is all the commotion? Who's doing all that dang infernal shooting? You're actin' worse than a bunch of wild Indians. A man can't get any sleep with all this claptrap." The voice belonged to a long-bearded, longhaired old man emerging over the top of the Butte.

"Suppose you tell us who you are, or you'll find out just how good a shot I am," Running-water said.

Unfazed by Running-water's threat, the white head continued to climb over the top of the Butte. When he got to his feet he said, "Been a long time since anybody's been out here. I see you got rid of those pesky rattlers. Good thing."

"Why is that so?" Esaugetuh said.

"They were gettin' too bossy. Always hanging around the only water supply out here. Say, you doin' some kind an initiation? That one," he said pointing at Adam "looks like some creature from another time. Oh well, we get all kinds of weirdoes out here from time to time."

"I don't know. I just live here."

78

"What do you mean you don't know?" Everybody knows who they are?" Running-water snapped.

"Well I don't and that's that. Besides, I never met anybody who was as they claimed. There's always something left unrevealed. You gonna eat all them rattlers?"

"You are welcome to some of them. Take your pick. Care to sit a spell?" Esaugetuh said motioning to a spot on the ground next to him.

The old man squatted down, selected three of the snakes, and within minutes had them skinned. Like Esaugetuh had instructed Running-water, the old man rolled up the skins into tight little bundles.

"They'll make good shoes. Thank you kindly."

Esaugetuh watched the old man intently. There was something about him. Esaugetuh just couldn't let it go. Some forgotten memory struggled to surface. Straining to see, he squinted, trying to force the memory into view.

"You've been out here for a while?" Esaugetuh asked.

"I think so. Here days melt into one another; an endless seam. I get up, take a piss, eat, walk around, maybe take a crap, and do the same thing all over again."

Running-water perked up at that point. He looked at the unkempt old derelict and that what he was. "No," he thought, "he's a desert rat."

"Who's the fella covered with mud? He sick. I smell sage and heuchera. Both make a good poultice."

"I am Adam. The old one is my father, Esaugetuh; the other is my friend, Running-water. This is a sacred place, a place of power. I am here to get over an illness." He peeled away another layer of the backed on poultice.

"Did you say Running-water?"

"Yes. He is—,"

"Your soul mate."

"Yes. But how do you know that?" Adam said.

"I-I don't know. Just popped into my head."

"You live here among the buttes? How do you manage? I see no weapons," Adam said.

"There's a small cave around the back of this Butte. I live there. I use snares and traps to catch animals. Some of the vegetation is edible. Always the questions. Never the answers, eh?"

"Besides my father, only one other person said that to me. Does the name Jedediah Woods mean anything to you?" Adam asked.

"Can't say that it does. I got to admit, though, there's something familiar about you. Maybe I met somebody who was always asking questions."

"How about a log cabin with plowed fields?" Adam said.

"I think I may have lived in once. Not sure."

"Adam? What are you getting at?" You know my grandfather was electrocuted in Albuquerque," Running-water said. "It's just impossible that—,"

"Albuquerque? I think I may have lived there once. Something about it. Maybe? Just can't remember."

The sound of a helicopter cut off any further conversation. "Get the fire up. Make it blaze!" Esaugetuh shouted.

Running-water began tossing the remainder of the cactus cast onto their fire. As each hit, it burst into short-lived flames. Pausing between each toss to give added emphasis to their signal and to make it last longer, Running-water hoped it was enough for the chopper to see them.

[1] Algonquian language
[2] Fa-nays. Greek mythology.
[3] Information on preparing the rattlesnake is from the website of Brazos River Rattlesnake Ranch, Texas.

CHAPTER NINE

A helicopter flooded the Butte with a high beam of light. Another beam turned the night into day as a second chopper flew low over the four men. The old man, shaking his fist, tried to wave them off. Running-water clobbered him. A miniature dust storm swelled up as the huge Bell helicopter landed. Before its blades stopped, Brett and Samuel jumped out and ran toward the outcropping. Samuel immediately began yelling, "Adam! I'm coming!

For a man of his size, Samuel moved with complete agility. It was a strange sight to see this hulk galloping through space. He used his size to pole-vault to the top of the small Butte. Long ago, he learned that once you get a heavy object moving, its momentum increases. Shocked by Adam's appearance, Samuel stopped his bellowing and stood perfectly still. Brett, right behind him, with mouth agape, expelled air in disbelief. Adam's appearance stunned Dutch, who was the last to join the rescue group. It was difficult to say who was more surprised, Dutch, or Adam. "I'm sure I saw my father kill him." Adam thought, shaking his head to clear the image of memories. "I must be hallucinating!"

"No, my brother, you are not. We are being rescued," Running-water replied to Adam's thoughts. He misunderstood Adam's comment.

"Be on your guard. Stay close. Bring the old man with us. Brett and Samuel are to travel with us. Let's get out of here."

"You know something I don't."

"No more telepathy. Just be on your guard."

As soon as everyone was on board and secured in their seats the Bell lifted off and then circled around the Butte and headed south. Esaugetuh and the old man were engaged in whispered conversation. Brett rode shotgun at the back of the pilot's cabin. Opposite from him sat the ever-watchful Running-water. He was paying particular attention to the second smaller chopper flying along their right side. Dutch violated his orders to stay with the jet. And then there was the question of the whereabouts of Will Rexford. He had not been with Dutch on the Butte and yet, there he was sitting next to Dutch. Samuel sat facing Adam, who was in an awake-sleep, eyes unblinking and focused on some invisible spot.

Samuel thought of speaking to Adam but was reluctant to do so. He waited and watched. That was his job, to watch over Adam. He took it literarily. "Somehow I've failed. I got to make it up to Adam. It's my fault that he nearly died. I should have been smart enough to know that the last of the remaining Brothers, Paul, and Phillip had set a trap for him. Any idiot would have known the so-called 'security-field' they had created was a beacon for the She-Devil, a beacon to direct her attack on Adam. Man, talk about stupid. I am that." Samuel sighed. Filled with remorse and shame, he leaned forward again to check on Adam.

It was then that he heard. He shook his head to make sure he was indeed hearing Adam.

"Easy my friend. Quiet your thoughts. You are not to blame yourself. I am the one who trusted Phillip and Paul. Samuel, talk to me about the Gatlin guns? From where did they come? Who brought them to the monastery?"

Samuel, uncertain about his ability to mind-talk looked at Adam for reassurance. Adam placed a finger over his lips and then touched Samuel's forehead. Samuel nodded his head in understanding. They were to continue using telepathy.

"Dutch and Will Rexford. Not sure where they got them. I think one of them mentioned something about an uncle."

Adam nodded and gave Samuel an ok sign. He wondered why the charges from the Gatlin guns hadn't killed Moon-Woman. " One thing for sure, they sure charged her up. "Hmm. Maybe that's what they were supposed to do," he thought.

Dutch took the accompanying chopper, a Schweizer 300, directly above the Bell. Then he dropped back down to their level. Adam looked out the window and could easily see Dutch at the controls and Will Rexford in the seat next to him. He wondered how that could be. Hadn't Esaugetuh killed him with a blast from a shotgun? A slight shudder gave away his discomfort. He just couldn't get a handle on why he thought they were dead. If it wasn't all hallucinations, maybe it was a vision, a harbinger of things to come. That thought unnerved him. He felt the hair on the nap of his neck move.

Adam straightened up in his chair, leaned forward as far as the seatbelt would allow. "Brett, tell our pilot that the next time our friends zooms above us that he is immediately to go full throttle straight ahead and to maintain acceleration until told to do otherwise."

With the ease of the expert he was, Dutch shot the small chopper high above the whirling blades of the Bell-427. The Bell shot forward, banked to the right, hovered for a minute, and then roared full speed at the smaller chopper. The pilot of the Bell did a quick maneuver and came up alongside Dutch.

Adam had the pilot patch him through to Dutch. "Knock it off! You know I don't like aircraft flight above me," Adam said. His voice was weak. He remembered a past time when another plane had tried to knock his jet out of the sky by landing on top of it. Dutch knew that. He had been the pilot of his jet." Maybe that's what was making me uneasy." It didn't do any good to pretend that was the reason. It ran deeper than that. Adam searched his memory bank, trying to remember what it was that was out of place. Dutch interrupted his thoughts.

"Just playing tag, boss man. Don't get your shorts in a twist."

"Grow up will you!" Running-water interrupted.

"Have our pilot move out. As soon as we land, we'll board the jet. Put Brett in as the pilot. Radio ahead to have the plane made ready and get emergency clearance for departure," Adam said.

After a brief whispered conversation with the pilot, the Bell-427 shot forward. The sudden burst of speed took Dutch by surprise. He knew he could not maintain a high speed and still have enough fuel to reach the airport. By slowing to a cruising speed of seventy he could conserve his fuel. The Bell ate the distance with ease. As soon as it touched down, Adam and his group boarded his Gulfstream. Brett eased the jet out onto the runway, waited for his turn to take off. Within minutes, they were airborne and headed to Bellingham, Washington.

They had not been airborne for long when Brett heard the familiar voice in his headset.

"Hey Brett, what the hell's going on? Why didn't the boss man wait for us?

"Hey Dutch. Where are you?" Brett replied.

"We're just landing at Flagstaff. What the big rush, man? Better turn around and come get us."

"This is Running-water. We are not coming back to pick you up. You are fired. You'll find a notice of your dismissal and a severance check waiting for you at the main desk in the terminal."

"That's not funny. You can't fire me. Adam hired me. What about Will? You firing him, too?"

"Read your contract fly-boy. Will is not our employee," Running-water said as he hit the off button ending the conversation.

Turning to Brett, he said, "I'm going back and inform Adam. Are y okay for a while?"

"No problem. When you come back, mind telling me what's with Dutch and Will?" Brett said.

"That will be up to Adam."

Running-water's tone told Brett that he was not to ask about Dutch and Will again. The tension between Adam, Dutch, and Running-water bothered him. "Something happened to piss Adam off. Dutch and me have been through a lot together. I think he would have said something about it. Will Rexford's another story. Wonder if he and Dutch are lovers? Maybe that's why Dutch left the military. I always figured him a career man. I've never had any indication that either Adam or Running-water was homophobic. "

A voice from the control tower at the Bellingham airport brought him back into focus. He banked the Gulfstream into a holding pattern. Waited until the voice gave him clearance to land.

The Gulfstream landed smoothly and taxied to its designated hanger. Thirty minutes later, the door opened and the steps lowered. One person hurried down the steps and disappeared into the hanger. The giant doors slowly opened, and a stretch limousine eased its way out of the darkened hangar. It stopped near the plane's steps.

Samuel heaved himself out of the driver's seat, closed the door, and stood waiting. People in the tower watched with fascination. Even though they were accustomed to seeing private planes come and go, this one held their attention. It was the only one with an eagle's head painted on its tail. Because of their preoccupation with the plane, none of them saw the shotgun hanging at the side of the chauffeur

First of the plane were two old men, each slightly bent. Even so, one was taller than the other was. They hesitated for a moment, assessing their surroundings, before descending the steep steps. Shortly after they entered the waiting limo, a man with long blue-black hair appeared in the doorway.

It wasn't just his good looks that attracted the attention; it was the Uzi he carried. He paused, surveyed the surroundings, nodded to Samuel, turned back into the plane, and emerged with someone wrapped from head to toe in a blanket. Bare feet and legs moving beneath the blanket were noticeably visible.

The driver helped the blanket figure into the waiting limousine. Sliding in behind the steering wheel, Samuel drove a distance from the plane, stopped and waited. The plane was towed into the hanger; it's nose facing out. The giant doors rolled shut; coming together with a loud thud. Shortly another young man emerged through a side door. He stopped, checked that it was locked and then joined the longhaired man standing by the stretch limo. Both hurriedly jumped into the limo. With its tires squealing, the limo sped out of the airport.

For thirty minutes, it headed south. During that time, no one spoke. Samuel's voice broke the silence. "Adam. There's a call for you. Do you want to take it?"

"Who is it?" Adam said.

"Says his name is Gordon, Gordon Rapport."

"You take the call," Adam said to Running-water. "And say nothing about me."

The conversation was brief. When Running-water asked Adam why he hadn't wanted to talk with Gordon Rapport, Adam said he'd explain things all in good time. That didn't satisfy Running-water, but he kept his silence. "I don't understand why Adam didn't want to talk to my uncle," Running-water thought. "He's been there to help

88

us. Didn't he help us find a pilot and navigator when the first two tried to kill us? I just don't get it. Adam's voice has become gravelly; not much different from the Wisdom Keeper. I wonder if he's gone over to the Other Side?"

Adam's voice brought him to quick attention.

"I wonder if Gordon still has those videotapes of us at Mesa Verde? You remember those?" Adam said.

"Tapes? No. I'm sure I'd turned over the tape I had to the Rez paper I was working for. What made you think of my interview with you?" Running-water said.

"Can't rightly say," Adam replied.

He hated to lie to Running-water. And that's what it was, a lie. Since Running-water didn't recall making the videotapes showing nearly every move Adam and Esaugetuh had made while at the conference at the Mesa that left Gordon Rapport. The tapes were in Albuquerque at the apartment that Gordon and Running-water shared from time to time. "Why would he want to videotape Esaugetuh and me? In fact, Rapport first mentioned them. Strange," Adam thought.

The silence that permeated the atmosphere was nearly as heavy as the armored limo itself as it sped along I-5 south. Even the old men were quiet.

CHAPTER TEN

Looking out one of the massive windows on the third floor of The Monastery, Adam silently watched the darkening clouds. Darkened with anger, they fought one another for dominance. Larger dark foreboding clouds smashed into lighter clouds—swallowing them. Unlike most storms, this one had no thunder or streaked lightening. Just angry, rolling clouds. He pulled open the window and stepped out on the balcony. No wind; not even a gentle breeze. Looking at the massive buildup, Adam wondered what had caused such anger. And like those clouds, his anger had been building. First, it was shock; then disappointment, and then the anger.

He did not direct his anger at his father, Esaugetuh, or his soul mate, Running-water, nor was it directed at his beautiful Daphne, mother of his four sons. It was inner anger and the cancer it was, ate at him. It was anger caused by his misjudgment—his misjudgment of character—a personal flaw, he found intolerable.

"I should have known The Brothers were not to be trusted. After all, I'm supposed to be able to read people's thoughts, to see into their souls. I gave them my trust, respect, and friendship. Even Running-water did not fully grasp their evil. He is not to blame. My father had not realized their betrayal until it was nearly too late. Is the object lesson here to be suspicious of everyone? Where is the compassion in that?"

"You don't pick up a rattler and stroke it after it has bitten you. You have not followed the old tradition of an eye for an eye. You did not seek revenge. You protected yourself and your family," Esaugetuh said joining his son on the balcony.

"Notice there is no thunder or lightning within the storm clouds," Adam said as he turned to greet his father.

"They reflect you. What is it that troubles you, my son?"

"I have held my thoughts on several issues. I need to know what happened on the Gulfstream when we landed at Flagstaff. When you and Running-water were taking me off the plane, I saw you shoot and kill Will Rexford. I saw you knife Dutch Masters, and I watched him die. How is it that they are still alive?" Adam said.

"I don't know what demons possessed you at that time, but I did not kill your pilot or his friend. Are you sure, it was me? Was it a twin of yourself? Maybe someone else? We live our lives in imagination, and it is possible that you experienced a shift in reality. Sometimes in such cases, appearances can be deceiving. Can you remember other things you saw?" Esaugetuh said. He put his arm around Adam's shoulder trying to comfort his distraught son.

"I have traveled where others have not. I have walked among the dead as well as the living dead. I have watched souls being sorted. I have traveled beneath the earth, and I have been thrust at breakneck speed back out into the universe. There, I looked into the vortex and saw transcendence, and I have wandered in the Akasha but this-this is something different," Adam said.

"We continually live in different aspects of our perceived realities and their fluctuating time intervals. Those who have walked before us have said that events of life are first seen as potentialities; then they become realities. Such revelations are the purpose of Dreamtime. The secret to understanding and interpreting these revelations involves knowing human nature. Is destiny your concern?" Esaugetuh said.

"Are you suggesting I have seen the destiny of Dutch Masters and Will Rexford? That I have a near perfect photo montage of their deaths? That in some strange way, I have projected you and myself into the picture? If what you say is true, shouldn't I warn them of this?" Adam said

"Aren't you still suspicious of their behavior? Didn't you leave them in Flagstaff? Didn't Running-water fire Dutch?"

"Yes, I still have my questions, my suspicions about their behavior? But still, Old One shouldn't I—,"

"I most certainly would not!"

"Why not? My god, I owe them a least that much. Surely, if we can see the future we ought to be able to change it," Adam said.

"You may not have the whole picture. I strongly urge you to hold off telling them anything. What you believe you saw may have some other meaning, and if it does, then what? Telling them would certainly ruin whatever joy they find in this life. No one wants to know they are going to die even though they know it is inevitable."

"You're right. I don't know enough. Tell me, father, have you ever experienced these fluctuations in reality? Many times in the past, I felt we were so close and yet so totally apart, in different worlds so to speak."

"How do you feel?"

"What? I don't understand." Adam said.

"I'm asking you how you feel, not what you feel. And don't give me a flip answer and say with your hands."

"I seem to sense things with my whole body. It's as though I am like the Antennae Galaxies, picking up thoughts from everywhere and all at once, myriads of feelings and emotions colliding just as those clouds are colliding?" Adam said pointing out toward the sky.

"Each of us belongs to a different aspect of those processes that govern all things. Your sons, Indigos, are just one such example. They, as well as you and I, are a part of the vast and endless diversity existing within the human race, within the world, and within the cosmos. It seems to me that each person has a particular purpose in the exploration of the different dimensions of human potentiality. I think you are still trying to sort out yours," Esaugetuh said.

"Are you saying we are different from others?"

"Yes. We are different, you and me, your children. An ancient philosopher, barely mentioned in the history of things, named Monoimus has said 'we should begin looking within ourselves as the starting point to find out who is within, who makes everything his own." [1] Perhaps that is what you ought to do," Esaugetuh said.

"You mean another vision quest? I don't want to go off into the mountains and leave my family. I've left them enough as it is. Isn't there something else I can do?"

"Maybe. A few have the ability to penetrate other dimensions. You have done that and I suppose you can do it again. If you decide to do that, be very careful. I don't know if Moon-Woman had influence in that area or not."

"She is no more. Have no fear about that. However, you seem to feel that there is still a danger. I sense it is more so than when I mind-walked a parallel universe in my search for you?" Adam said.

"Don't you remember? There is another Self who creates your personal reality. That's why I told you there can only be one. Don't tell me you have forgotten?" Esaugetuh said.

"I have not. I just don't see the connection," Adam replied.

"It is the Soul that creates your true Self and it is possible for you to lose it. An evil force could capture it, and with your powers that would be most unfortunate. There's always the possibility that your soul could be stolen during a walk in a different dimension," Esaugetuh said. His voice quivered.

"You have forgotten, father. I have a soul-mate. He will look after my soul. Besides, my sons grow in their abilities daily. They are an additional source of power. And of course, I have you," Adam said.

"So be it. I'll help you, but you must at all times remember that the notion of multiple minds is an illusion, that is, there is but one mind and it sees both the light and the dark; [2] it is simultaneously both. And it can trick you and steal your soul," Esaugetuh said.

"I wonder if Christine Lilith Conduit is available. She is very good with dual hypnotism. I'll ask Running-water to track her down and see if she will come here. I sense this time there will be a crossing over. In the meantime, what should I be doing in preparation?"

"Preparation has to be personal and private. Unlike before when you went upon your Vision Quest I cannot help you. Purify yourself, cleanse your mind, and refresh your soul. Follow the old ways when calling upon the Spirits. Render respect; behave with dignity, and above all demand nothing. Make peace with yourself. Remember whatever you do, it is reflected throughout the universe," Esaugetuh said.

He left Adam on the balcony and went inside. He thought it best to leave his son alone, to give him some space and time to think. He noticed the dark clouds had moved on over the mountain. That was a good sign.

[1] The original statement as reported by Hippolytus in Refutation of All Heresies, book 8 is 'Omitting to seek after God, and creation and things similar to these, seek for Him (out of) thyself and learn who it is that absolutely appropriates (unto Himself) all

things in these, and says, "My god, my mind, my understanding, my soul, my body.' And learn from whence sorrow and joy, and love, and hatred, and involuntary wakefulness and involuntary drowsiness, and involuntary anger, and involuntary affection, and if you accurately investigate these (point), you will discover (God) Himself, unity and plurality, in thyself, according to that life, and that He finds the outlet (for Deity) to be from thyself."

[2] Fred Alan Wolf. Dr. Quantum Presents a User's Guide to Your Universe. Sounds True Audio Learning Course 6CD's. Boulder. Co. 2006. A paraphrase of Dr. Wolf's statement.

CHAPTER ELEVEN

After asking Running-water to locate Christine Lilith Conduit, Adam retired to a secure room below ground, a secret sanctuary. It contained no furniture. A tanned deerskin lay in the middle of the floor; beside it was an earthen dish. On the wall hung several bunches of dried herbs and other plants. From these, Adam selected dried sweet grass and sage. He lit the sage, wafted it around the small room, and then placed its remnants on the earthenware dish where they burned out. The sage purified the room. Stripping off his clothes, he next lit the small bundle of sweet grass and smudged it over his body. He sat down on the deerskin and began a low-voiced chant.

Gradually he turned the chant into a humming. The place on his neck where the ancient Wisdom Keeper's obsidian amulet hung pulsed. Gradually the sound filled the room, vibrating off the walls and bathing him. There was a synchronizing of vibration and pulse. Slowly his muscles began to relax; his breathing steadied, and his heartbeat slowed. All Time stopped.

He felt good when he meditated. It brought him closer to his spiritual being. Whenever he opened his soul to sacredness, he felt warm and safe. He knew it would do no good to list his knowledge, to point out his virtues or his acts of healing, or to announce his victory over Moon-woman. A line from Kazantzakis steamrolled through his mind. *The highest point a man can attain is not knowledge or virtue, or goodness, or victory, but something even greater, more heroic, and more despairing: sacred awe!* [1] Don't brag and don't demand when it comes to the Spirits. One could ask and maybe, if judged worthy, they might grant the boon. That thought brought him face to face with one of his existential questions: What does worthy mean? The formation of that question shattered Adam's tranquility. He got up, took an elevator to the third floor.

Daphne was startled to see her husband stark naked. She managed to conceal her pleasure at seeing him naked. Their quadruplets, busy playing at their mother's feet, stopped their activity and stared at their father. Their vibrations told Adam they were talking about him. He tuned in.

"Don't worry, someday you will be as big as me," Adam said, bending down and scooping them up in his arms. Delighted with the attention, they giggled and the momentary intrusion displaced Adam's question. Once again, he relaxed.

The boys wanted to know why their mother had clothes on when he didn't. Adam told them that a lady kept her body clothed. "Someday," he said, "you'll have women of your own who will come to you naked. Respect that."

The door to their apartment opened, and Running-water walked in. He had contacted Christine Lilith Conduit, and she had agreed to come to the Monastery. "I've arranged to send the Gulfstream for her."

"Good. Did you take care of all the details?"

"Yes. You showing off again? Remember the fuss when Isha saw that nude photo of you? He ever tell you about that, Daphne?"

"Knock it off, will you?" Adam said as he gave Running-water an affectionate cuff aside of the head.

"You want me to have the guest rooms set up or do you want—,"

"Up here," Adam said, cutting him off

"What secrets are you two cooking up now?" Daphne said.

"I'm going on a trip, and Christine Lilith Conduit is coming here to help me do that. She is a nationally known hypnotist who channels. She tried to help me locate Esaugetuh by using dual hypnotic trance. She will try to help me travel in another dimension. I have planned a surprise for my father. I can't tell you because he may tune into your thoughts and find out beforehand," Adam said.

"I don't know much about this mind-travel business. It seems I read somewhere that it's dangerous. What if you can't come back? I want to go with you." Daphne said.

"Not possible."

"Why are you going? Where are you going?" Daphne said. Her eyes flashed the anger that was building.

"I am that I am."

And that's the way it always was. Daphne smarted under his lack of confiding in her. The old haunt came back to nag at her. "Am I nothing more than the receptacle for his seed. The boys are not our sons; they are his sons."

Breaking her thoughts, she said to Running-water, "Leave us. I want to talk to Adam."

Running-water knew when his sister was really pissed. He quickly headed toward the elevator.

"I have a question for you, Adam. Am I not your wife? If I am, then this hush-hush crap is to stop. I don't know where you have been, naked as you are, but your whereabouts will no longer be secretive. Either take me into your confidence, totally and completely or find yourself another place to camp out. And I don't mean here. And another thing; the boys are not just your sons. They are our sons. Your semen wouldn't have been worth shit if I hadn't had four eggs ready to be fertilized."

"My providing for you is not enough?" Adam said. His voice was quiet and controlled.

"No, it is not!"

"My protecting you is not enough?"

"No!"

"And my loving you is not enough?"

"No!"

"What is it, you want from me?"

"Trust. Have you forgotten your own words?" Daphne said. She broke into tears.

Adam pulled her to him, wrapped his arms around her, and let her finish her cry. Internal wisdom told him it was best to keep quiet. Realizing that there wasn't a rebuttal coming from him, Daphne looked up at him. Searching his azure blue eyes, she looked for an answer. He kissed her, holding it, filling it with his longing for her. When he released the kiss, he whispered, " I do trust you with all that I am."

Running-water returned. They were standing together, wrapped in each other, oblivious of all else. From the elevator, he could see Adam's manliness pushing against his sister's thigh. He pushed the button closing the elevator door.

[1] Nikos Kazantzankis' Zorba the Greek. Simon & Schuster. New York. 1996 50th Anniversary Edition The italics are the authors.

CHAPTER TWELVE

After they had spent themselves, Daphne began to rise up. Adam held her down and taking her beautiful face in his hands said, "You have to try to understand."

"Understand? Understand what?"

"A man says, 'my sons' and does so with pride. That does not take away from the mother. To her, they are her babies, and I understand they always will be. Not so for a man. They are his sons. It's a man's way. There is no intent to diminish the role of the mother. It would be the same if our children were girls. They would be my daughters."

She was silent. He looked at her searching for some sign of acceptance.

"As far as trust is concerned, I trust you completely. I have some serious misgivings about certain people in our extended family. I have to be very careful not to make false accusations. Not even your brother is aware of this. My father is. It is for this reason I have sent for Christine Lilith Conduit. She is going to help me mind-walk in another time to find specific evidence or the lack of evidence for my feelings. I have been betrayed enough. I have not told you this before because you and Running-water mind-talk, and I do not want him to know just yet. I don't want to hurt him in any way. And he will be if I call into question his judgment regarding certain issues. He will know all in good time. You must promise me that you will not dwell on what I have just told you," Adam said.

"What if it pops into my head?"

"Simply say to yourself 'what is my next thought?' It will erase your current thoughts."

She knew he was right. What good would come of a premature accusation? She would practice what he said. "I've got to go," she whispered as she eased herself from him.

He went to his bathroom, shaved his head, leaving a pile of his long dark hair on the marble floor. Next, he shaved his face, his armpits, and then his pubic hair. He then showered. With great care, he searched in his herbals' cabinet until he found the right tincture. He selected tincture of bloodstone and mixed a few drops with eucalyptus oil in a small bottle. He shook it until he was satisfied that the mixture had emulsified. Then he rubbed the mixture over his hairless body. He felt the shamanic tattoo on his wrist pulsate. He watched the bolt of lightning that ran across the eagle's feather. He was sure it was flickering. Whenever it acted up, and that's what he called it, he had the distinct sensation that something was about to happen. Generally, it was a warning. And experience taught him to heed such a warning.

Adam dressed and went to his wife's bath to check on her. She was not there. He found her curled up with their sons on the floor of their huge living room. All were asleep. He checked each of the boys and then bent down, kissed Daphne. He was relieved that they were okay. His thoughts turned to Running-water, his wife, Isha, and their twins. Instead of taking the elevator to the next floor below him, he raced down the stairs, ran down the hall to their apartment. Not bothering to knock, he burst into their living room. No one was there. He stopped at their bedroom, listened, but heard nothing. He went to their sons' room. Once again, he listened. And again, he heard nothing. Concern mapped all over his face. He called out their names. The massive drapes moved at one of the large center windows. Running-water stuck his head in. "We're out here on the balcony. What's up?"

"Man, you had me worried. Is everything okay here?" Adam said.

"Sure. We're watching the Old One. He seems to be building something. Something wrong?" Running-water said.

"Maybe just a premonition but I have a feeling that something is not right. Have you seen Samuel and Julie, Patricia, or Dr. Bach?"

"No. I haven't seen any of them today," Running-water replied. "Brett's off to get your packages."

"Hmm. Have you had any communication from Dutch Masters or Will Rexford?"

"Not since I fired Dutch. You're really spooked. Let's check security. I'll go with you."

As they walked down the flight of stairs, Adam stopped, turned, and looked at Running-water. "Have you heard anything from your uncle Gordon or Cornelia, your mother?"

"Nothing from either of them. Man, you sure are spooked. What's got you so uptight? When I last saw you and Daphne the two of you were getting it on hot and heavy," Running-water said.

"Wish I knew, my brother. Wish I knew. It hangs over me, a heavy shadow."

They found Samuel at the control center on the first floor. He was monitoring the security system. After a review of the premises via closed-circuit television, Adam insisted that Samuel change all the codes for the whole security system; inside and out. Once those were in place Adam and Running-water went to check on Dr. Bach. He was not in. They found Patricia Livingston at her computer. Julie was in her kitchen making bread.

"I want the compound checked for explosives," Adam said.

Running-water whipped out his cell phone, punched in a number for a security company in Bellingham. It took some explaining by Running-water to get the company's dispatch to understand where they were to bring the sniffer-dogs. Even though the place is now Eagles' Crest people, who lived in the surrounding areas still referred to it as The Monastery. The dispatch knew the location.

"Whatever happened to the security dogs we had at the house in Toronto?" Adam said.

"They are being boarded at a private kennel," Running-water replied.

"Have them shipped here and get someone to train them for this place," Adam said.

"I believe Samuel managed the dogs. If not, I'll find a trainer. You still have any idea about what's gotten you so spooked?"

"No."

"Well, I know this much. Whenever you get one of these moods, it generally means trouble is afoot. You want to start doing shifts. I'll take whichever one you don't want," Running-water said.

"Let's hold off on that until nightfall. No use upsetting our families. Have you seen the old man from the desert?"

"No."

Adam found his father and the old man whom he believed to be Jedediah Woods, Running-water's grandfather. Esaugetuh was busy and did not let on that he was aware of his son's approach. Adam squatted down, a short distance away. He watched his father and like the proverbial sponge, he soaked up every movement, every gesture, and every expression on his father's face. He marveled at the Old One's agility and stamina. Most of all he admired his father's ability to see through issues.

Without stopping his work and without looking up, Esaugetuh said, "You'll need to prepare yourself over a period of seven days. What you are about to undertake is doubly dangerous since you have done it once before. Sometimes the Spirits don't take kindly to such intrusions."

"What are you making?" Adam asked, ignoring his father's concern.

"A tiponi," [1] Esaugetuh said

"What's that?"

"Sometimes it's called the heart of a ceremony; it's made of an ear of dried corn, feathers, and corn and vegetable seeds. They go in a clay base in much the same way your woman arranges a bouquet of flowers in a vase. I'm braiding some colored cloth to hang down the sides of the corn. You want to help?" Esaugetuh said.

"Sure. Tell me what you would have me do."

And Esaugetuh did. They busied themselves braiding the cloth, painting the base of the tiponi. Once it was painted and the cloth fringe securely tied to the dried ear of corn, Esaugetuh painted a silhouette of an eagle on the base. Carefully, he turned the tiponi around, examining each detail. A grunt was his signal of approval.

"What do you do with it?" Adam asked.

"It is put at the center of a reredo as an offering to the Spirits," Esaugetuh replied.

"Reredo? I've not heard of that before. What is it?" Jedediah said.

"Now who's asking the questions?" Adam teased. The three of them laughed.

"It's a standalone screen, similar to some used in Christian churches. It stands behind an altar. The one I am making is made of cedar slats and baked clay tiles. The symbols of the sun, moon, clouds, lightning, and eagles will decorate the tiles. I have mixed some of the dyes to color the clay. I borrowed some of the bricks from one of your outbuildings to make an oven. Hope you don't mind," Esaugetuh said.

"What may I do to help?" Jedediah asked. He was anxious about being left out. He wondered why Running-water was not helping. "Seems to me my grandson ought to be out here.

"You can be the keeper of the fire. The wood chips must be kept red hot, but no flames," Esaugetuh said.

"And me? What do you want me to do?" Adam asked.

"Make the tiles. Make them square or round. Use different dyes for bricks. Seven batches of the clay have been prepared. Add the dyes as you need them."

"Once they are baked, where do you want them?" Adam asked.

"When they have cooled, glue them to that four-foot long box I've already made. It will be the actual altar," Esaugetuh said.

At the day's end, the three of them had a beautiful reredo and tiled altar. The altar bricks were the colors of the cardinal directions. Esaugetuh had decided he would complete making a sacred place for his son's preparation for his presentation to the spirit world in the morning. Trudging back to the Monastery, he felt at peace knowing the traditions were honored. That was one of the things he appreciated about Adam; he honored the traditions even though a white man had raised him.

The sun surrendered its command to night clouds. Adam briefed Samuel on his decision to set up shifts. Samuel would take the first shift, Running-water the second, and Adam would take the third. Samuel suggested a back-up security system if both the electric power and the battery systems failed. Using a large number of old cowbells from the barn, Samuel strung those a short distance from the doors and windows of the ground floor. Anyone moving in those areas would get entangled and create a racket.

The property was relatively secure; one gated road led up to the compound, a sheer granite cliff protected the backside of the property. Aware they were vulnerable from the air, Adam moved the members of his household to the lower levels below ground. Patricia Livingston, Julie, Isha, and her twins also moved to the lower levels. Esaugetuh and Jedediah Woods refused to go to a safe-room and insisted they have a turn. They opted for the roof. Two members of the compound were not present. Brett had flown the Gulfstream back east to get Christine Lilith Conduit; Dr. Allan Bach was nowhere to be found. It was assumed he had hitched a ride into town with Brett and was spending the night with a woman friend.

[1] Much of the information regarding the tiponi and the reredo is based on Thomas E. Mails' Secret Nature American Pathways: A Guide to Inner Peace. Council Oak Books. Tulsa, OK., 1988. The author has modified some aspects of an actual tiponi and reredo to fit his story line.

CHAPTER THIRTEEN

Dawn was a most welcome beacon. The night passed without incident. Even the two old men stationed on the roof slept peacefully. With the sunrise, they awoke, stretched, lowered their rope ladder, and climbed down the three stories. Both, too stubborn to admit it, were glad to plant their feet firmly on the ground. Peace seemed to be the order of the day except for Adam. His unease continued to gnaw at his gut, a wretched foreboding engulfing him. This morning he took no food.

He went outside, climbed on board an ATV, and began a tour of the 100-acre compound. Frequently, he stopped and listened. The birds and squirrels had grown used to the human element and ignored him. Two brazen gray squirrels scolded him for intruding on their breakfast. He looked for footprints, broken branches or trampled foliage. He found none. Everything seemed normal; too normal. As he returned to the Monastery, he looked up at its roofline. And that reminded him that his father had said he would finish the altar this morning. Adam drove to the back of the main building.

In front of the reredo, Esaugetuh placed the tiponi. Seated on a square of tanned leather sat a medicine bowl. It was made of gold. Small delicate figures carved in raised relief adorned its sides. The figures could have been Mayan or Egyptian. The series of petroglyphs could just as well have been early Celtic. As Adam looked at the bowl, there was a strange familiarity about it. Fanning out from the bowl were seven radiating lies made of dried kernels of corn creating a sun.

Interrupting the two workers, Adam asked, "What are the lines?"

"Six represent the cardinal directions: North, South, East, West, Up, and Down," Esaugetuh replied.

"And the seventh?"

"The seventh represents the human soul or spirit," Esaugetuh said.

The detail his father had given to his project, impressed Adam. He noted at the end of each line of corn kernels was a colored feather whose color corresponded to the colors of the cardinal directions. North was yellow, South was green, East was white, and West was blue. Above was black and below was by orange. The seventh line was bright red.

"And what are those?" Adam said pointing to a row of colored sticks.

"Paaho Sticks. Prayer sticks are made of ears of dried corn, sticks, feathers, and beads." Adam noticed each complimented the colors of the cardinal directions. "When it is time, you will offer a prayer to the Spirits at each," Esaugetuh said.

"It will be as you wish, father. Did you or Jedediah have any problems during your watch?"

"All was quiet. You're still concerned. Since we didn't hear any alarms go off, I assume all was quiet," Jedediah said. It was the first he had acknowledged Adam's presence. "Just remember, I know how to use a shotgun."

The mention of shotgun brought back memories for Adam. He gave a shotgun to Jedediah at his log cabin farm in Pennsylvania. Only the real Jedediah would have known that. He decided since his father had accepted this man as Running-water's grandfather he felt there wasn't any reason not to accept him.

"Yeah," Adam replied, "I thought for a time you were going to blow the sheriff's head off."

"And I would have. I thought it was someone coming back to finish off my grandson. Speaking of him, have you seen that scallywag?" Jedediah said.

"No. Not this morning."

"We are nearly finished here. It might be a good time for you to get ready. Are you fasting? Have you cleansed yourself? I've gathered fresh herbs for you if you haven't," Esaugetuh said.

"I am fasting and I have cleansed myself. I appreciate the fresh herbs. Thank you."

It surprised Adam that his father had not mentioned his shaved head. He wanted to be clean inside and out and that meant no food, liquids, or body hair. "Damn! Daphne and I shouldn't have had sex. Too late now." A smile appeared at the corner of his lips. And that renewed his desire. Adam tried to refocus. His mind had to be clear of any physical desire when he approached the Spirits. Approaching them with lust in his heart would be insulting.

"Old One? Will you join me in my prayers? I would appreciate it if you were my guide as I present myself."

Esaugetuh looked at his son; turned to make an adjustment on one of the Paaho Sticks. He was

112

inwardly pleased but didn't wish to let his emotions show. "I will do as you ask," Esaugetuh said.

"Thank you, Jedediah, for your help in preparing my prayer altar. I must ask you to leave us now. From this point on my father and I must be alone."

Once Jedediah was inside, Adam stripped off his clothes, placed them in a basket. As Adam knelt down before the medicine bowl, Esaugetuh gave him an eagle-wing bone. Adam whistled directly into the bowl. It was a direct appeal to the Spirits to listen to his prayers. He then went to each of the seven Paaho Sticks, offering up a pipe filled with a mixture of sweet lemongrass, sage, and kinnikinic. He returned to the medicine bowl and again blew on the eagle-wing bone. From high above him, an eagle answered.

Adam repeated this seven times. And each time he heard the voice of the eagle. Looking up into the clear blue sky, he counted seven eagles spiraling upward and then fanning out. Just for a moment, he thought the Blue Angels could take a lesson from these magnificent birds. Esaugetuh touched him on a shoulder, nodded for him to go to the altar. Once in front of the altar, Esaugetuh gave Adam a spring of Asafetida.

"Burn it and smudge its smoke over your body," Esaugetuh said. Adam obeyed. Once he had smudged the smoke of the Asafetida, Adam walked over to a small basket, opened it, and pulled out a clean set of clothes. He pulled his shirt over his head. Running-water was standing in front of him.

113

"I am not to be left out of this, my brother," Running-water said, picking up another piece of Asafetida, lighting it, and smudging both. He pulled off his shirt and handed it to Adam, indicating that he was to give him his shirt. And so it went until they had exchanged clothes with each other. This bonding ceremony renewed them as inseparable brothers; their soulness reaffirmed each would have the other's support.

Esaugetuh who had watched this sharing was pleased with his choice. It was good to have brought the two of them together. He started to speak to them, changed his mind. Perhaps this is not the time to tell them. Let them stay as they are for a while longer.

CHAPTER FOURTEEN

Samuel was bellowing. "They're here!" Adam was sure everyone down in the small village could hear him.

First out of the SUV was a silver-haired woman. Using her silver-knobbed cane as a prod, she poked at Samuel; directing him to get her luggage from the back of the vehicle. For Samuel, it was "Yes ma'am" all over the place. The artist, the painter of souls as Adam had called her, had arrived. Genevieve Van Batten was dressed in skintight red leather pants, bolero top, red boots, and a truckload of sterling silver wrapped around her abdomen, neck, and wrists. The design suggested Navaho. Her red rouge accentuated high cheekbones; her lips, not to be outdone, were painted bright red, and were in a whimsical pout. Tucked under her arm was a long cardboard cylinder. She refused to allow Samuel to carry that. As she approached the massive white doors of the Monastery, she sensed someone was watching her. Stopping, she looked around; seeing no one, she hitched her butt only as a femme fatale could, and proceeded up the steps.

Christine Lilith Conduit exited next. Her disheveled carrot-red hair clashed with the outfit the old woman was wearing. It was an excellent statement of their short relationship. Besides that, she felt disheveled. Awakened at two in the morning by Brett's phone call telling her to pack a few things still didn't set well. She barely had time to brush her teeth before Brett whisked her away at breakneck speed. None of that made her happy. She thought she was to have a few days to get ready before he came to fly her to the west coast. Instead, Brett told her they would be flying to Burlington, Vermont. At the time, she thought Adam might be there since that was she had first met him.

Spending the night on a plane in a hanger was not her idea of accommodations. It had bothered her that she had to spend the night on the plane—alone. Despite Brett's gallant efforts to make her comfortable, she was not. She still remembered the prattle of a woman's voice and the sound of a slammed door. Wrapped in a white robe, she had left the luxurious bedroom and had gone forward. A mistake she now wishes she had not made. She was in the midst of preparing a summary of her research into dual hypnotic channeling and wanted to work on that. Brett's introduction was brief. The old woman's non-stop chattering made it impossible for her to work during their flight to Bellingham. Being polite to the old woman physically and emotionally drained her. Finally, in desperation, she escaped to the bedroom where she changed into her usual uniform of slacks, blouse, and jacket. She declined to eat breakfast with the old woman, feigning an upset stomach.

At the Monastery Christine Lilith Conduit was grateful the old woman had exited the SUV first. By the time, Samuel had returned to the SUV, she had retrieved her one small suitcase and had headed up the steps of the front portico. She thought it was odd that Samuel showed her a reception room; that

Adam did not greet her. She sighed. Relieved because Genevieve Van Batten was not there. She tried to make herself comfortable in the straight-back chair she was assigned to sit in. She resented being told to sit in a chair as if she were a naughty child. "I wonder where that Genevieve woman is. I'll be damned if someone is going to tell me where to sit." She got up. Stamped her foot. "I resent being ignored," she muttered.

She went to the large sliding double doors, determined to find out what was going on. Before she could give them a tug, they opened. Her mouth opened. She couldn't believe her eyes.

"Good lord is it really you?" she heard herself saying. "It can't be! You' re—,"

"Dead? Obviously not," Esaugetuh said. "Forgive me for sticking my nose into my son's affairs, but I want to speak to you about what it is, he is about. It concerns me. Both of us know that crossing over can be very dangerous. I'm not sure he's well enough to withstand the horrendous pressure such a journey will put upon him."

"You mean he wants to get more involved than astral projection?" Christine said

"Yes. Very much so, I'm afraid."

"Much more what?" Adam said as he entered the room. "I've been looking for you Old One. There's someone I want you to meet."

"We've already met and she agrees with me that what you want to do is very dangerous," Esaugetuh said. He was about to say more but was stopped by what he thought was an apparition, an image from another time.

"Well, you old coot, you just going to stand there with your mouth gaping?" Genevieve Van Batten said as she tossed a red-feathered boa over her shoulder. Despite her age, she still could come off as a vamp even if it was from a by-gone era. It brought her the desired results. An appreciative Esaugetuh had her in his arms, kissing her, his eyes filling with tears.

"Life is always ready for a new beginning," Esaugetuh said.

"And so it does. Where are those other very handsome young men you always have with you?" Genevieve asked, addressing Adam.

"Two of us are right behind you," Running-water said as he and Brett entered the great room.

"Still looking very much the man-killer, I see," Brett said, giving her a low, long whistle.

"Who's a killer?" Patricia Livingston said as she slipped into the great room with Daphne and Julie.

"Party time," Samuel said as he pushed a large cart filled with an array of finger foods. "Want me to open the bar?"

"Yes, but do not serve any to me," Adam said.

"And none for me?" Running-water said.

"What's going on?" Patricia Livingston said. She'd always be a reporter. It was in her blood. She simply could not refrain from asking questions.

"Adam, here, wants to take a trip. Christine, it might be better if you explained it," Esaugetuh said. He wrapped his arm around Genevieve's shoulder. It wasn't to protect her from what was about to be said, but rather to reassure himself.

118

"The human brain contains billions and billions of electrically active nerve cells called neurons. These direct and run our physical functions as well as our thought processes. Resonance amplifies these processes. If the individual's thought patterns are projections, then that individual travels dimensionally through time, past, and or future. Neurons can only burn glucose under normal conditions, consuming fifty percent of the blood sugar. However, if that process is disrupted normal metabolism disappears. The result is a vegetative state or death," Christine Lilith Conduit said.

"So, what's the problem?" Running-water asked.

"What Adam is proposing is an amplification of those processes through dual channeling to create a more powerful astral projection. Because of his recent illness and because he has done this once before, I cannot recommend doing it again. It's just too dangerous, too dangerous for both of us."

"I strongly disagree with you. My experience at traveling to another dimension should make this one easier and less strenuous because I know what to expect. We can use some post-hypnotic safeguards. Unlike before, I have my father and Running-water to serve as anchors. That will further lessen the strain," Adam said.

"I don't know," Christine said. "If we operate out of your circadian rhythm a cataclysmic change could take place destroying the both of us."

"Look, if you do not want to do this, I'll understand. Please accept my apology if you agreed to come here for some other purpose. You will be compensated for your time and any inconvenience the trip may have caused you," Adam said. His undertone said much more than his words. The anger was there, controlled as it was.

"Weren't you working on a book or something while we were on the plane?" Genevieve Van Batten said.

"A paper for an international symposium on paranormal psychology," Christine replied.

"And what was the topic of that paper?" Genevieve said. Her persistence caused Esaugetuh to look directly at her.

"Dual hypnotism as applied to astral projection. Where are you going with this?" Christine said.

"Well now, honey, it seems to me, you could use another direct experience, especially since you have such a willing subject," Genevieve said.

"Make that three willing subjects," Running-water said.

"This is totally out of hand. If I do this, and there a good chance I won't, only Adam, and I will be involved."

"You just don't get it. Adam and I are soul mates, soul brothers. We are spiritually joined. If something is done to one of us, it is done to the other. We have just completed a sacred ceremony reaffirming that. Old One, if this lady doesn't do as we wish, surely you know someone else who is equally well qualified," Running-water said. His irritation showed.

"When you have the best you don't look elsewhere. Christine, you and I go back a good number of years. We have not had the need to play silly games others play. What's the real issue for you?" Esaugetuh said.

Before answering, Christine looked first at Adam and then at Running-water. "How much alike they really are. You'd think they were actually twins. They even have the same speech pattern. Except for Adam's wondrous azure blue eyes, they truly could be brothers," she thought.

"Well?" Genevieve said. She tapped her foot showing her impatience.

"I was just thinking about how alike Adam and Running-water really are. They could be twins," Christine replied. "Have you ever noticed the similarities?"

"It's time you told them," Genevieve whispered to Esaugetuh as she gently squeezed his hand.

"They are!" Esaugetuh said. He didn't mean to say it that way; not just blurt it out like that. It was cold.

"Are what?" Christine said.

"Twins. Adam and Running-water are twins, and both are my sons. And now you know," Esaugetuh said. Turning to his stunned offspring, he continued, "I'm sure you want an explanation, and you will have one. But first, Christine, I remind you that you are indebted to me. I'm calling in that chip. Do as my sons ask."

The sharpness in his voice stunned Christine Lilith Conduit. In all the years, she had known him, worked conferences with him, and sat on scholarly panels with him; she had never heard him speak in such a harsh tone. True she owed him much, but to demand payment for something she felt he had freely given was an insult. "I'll be damned if I'm going to let him bully me. No man behaves that way toward me," she thought.

Before she could answer, Adam spoke up. "I have prepared myself. Let's get on with this." He showed no surprise at his father's announcement. He had wondered how it was that he and Running-water seemed so close, always seeming to know what the other was thinking, even before they had begun to telecommunicate.

"Yeah, let's get this over with. I've got other things to do. Can't wait around here all day," Running-water said. "Have you prepared yourself, father? I guess that's what I should call you from now on. Maybe, however, at your advanced age, you should sit this one out."

Running-water's sudden negative tone didn't register well with Christine. "Even if I had decided to do this, which I haven't, and I won't now under any circumstance. Negativism surrounds you. There is much anger here."

"It is as you say. There is much negativism and anger here. It surrounds your very being, Christine. You are angry because I reminded you of a past debt, actually taken offense that I brought it up. You have no reason to be. Running-water my question for you is: Why are you filled with negativism and anger?" Esaugetuh said.

"Yes, my brother, what bothers you?" Adam said.

"I've been manipulated and used. No one likes to be treated that way," Running-water said. His voice was full of bitterness.

"We went through all of this once before. I thought we had ended all of that. I released you from any sacred oath, you took on my behalf. At that time, I told you, you were free of me. I even sent you away. Yet, you chose to come back. I do not understand the source of your belligerency. Our bonding is short lived then. The sacred oaths we have taken this day no longer hold meaning for you. The sacrifices we have made for each other mean nothing?" Adam said.

Adam was about to say more but changed his mind. He remembered his father's words, 'there can be only one.' It occurred to him that Running-water was pissed because he wasn't a shaman. The room iced over. Adam slowly recognized that his soul-mate's disposition was more than a disgruntled pout.

Christine Lilith Conduit walked away from the group. She stopped in front of one of the large floor to ceiling windows that overlooked the expansive landscape. She did not see the beauty that lay before her—the elegant bronze eagle fountain and its sparkling water nor the myriad blooming flowers that populated the grounds. She wanted to go home. She was angry! Angry because she let the offer of a large sum of money sway her better judgment. "No. That's not it. It's— well, admit it. You hoped he might be available," she thought. She blushed as she remembered him sitting next to her, bare-assed naked. That was the time she used double hypnotic channeling with him. She patted her flushed face; sucked in her breath, exhaled slowly. She would return to Colorado. Adam can keep his money!

The all-pervasive negativity filling the room suffocated all conversations. Daphne and Patricia Livingston were stunned. Daphne didn't understand her brother's attitude. She was as shocked by Esaugetuh's news as he was, but she didn't see any reason for hostility. Genevieve Van Batten looked to Esaugetuh to do something. She realized, too late, that she should not have encouraged him to reveal the truth about his paternity. The thrill of being with Esaugetuh, shattered now, made her feel old and foolish. And she was!

On the second floor, Isha sensed that something was wrong. She immediately checked her twins and then the four babies of her sister-in-law. Lingering a bit to watch them, she noticed they no longer had the peculiar blue aura about them. It startled her; not having seen them without it. Grabbing the portable intercom monitor, she left the apartment. She ran down the long hallway to the elevator. She pushed the down button. Impatient for its arrival, she stamped her feet. It seemed to take forever for it to creak its way up to the second floor. Once inside, she pushed another button and the door closed. Unlike modern elevators, it was necessary to close the door and then select the floor. It began its slow creak to the first floor. She stared at the letters; each represented a level below ground. She'd not actually noticed them before. She was sure they had been there all along. The cage stopped. She hit the open button with exaggerated force. The door creaked open, and she hurried to the great room. She stopped and waited to be recognized. The cold emanating from within slapped her in the face.

No one looked at her or greeted her. It was rudeness, an insult not tolerated in the old days. She searched her husband's face for a clue as to what was wrong. She found seething anger. When she looked at Adam, she sensed deep remorse reflected in his azure blue eyes. The Old One was a blank. Daphne and Patricia Livingston sat off by themselves and the woman hypnotist, arms folded across her chest, was looking out a window.

"What is wrong? Someone say something!" Isha said sliding the doors closed.

"Ask the old man, the great Master of Breath," Running-water said. His voice was almost a low growl.

"I will answer," Adam said. "Running-water is angry at Esaugetuh; he is angry at me, and he is angry with himself." Esaugetuh has revealed that Running-water and I are twins, born of the same woman, created by the same man."

"My husband, why does this make you angry?" Isha said. "Your love for Adam has known no boundary. Often I have felt you cared more for him than you did our sons or me. If anyone should be angry, I should think it should be me. But I am not. And neither should you."

A barrage of gunfire at the front entrance stopped all conversation. Samuel stumbled through the door yelling, "I'm sorry Adam." The butt of an automatic weapon struck him. Blood oozing from his head, he slumped to the floor.

Two tall figures faces blackened and dressed in black, got off a round into the large mahogany sliding doors to the great room. The wood splintered. The first man shoved the doors open and shouted, "Nobody move!" He paused, looked around, and counted the number of people present. "Eight," he said into his mouthpiece.

"Who's missing?" The second figure said.

"I don't think anyone is missing," replied the first man.

"Where's the whore?"

"How in hell should I know? Let's get what we came for and get the hell out of here. This place creeps me out."

"All in good time. Where are the whore and the doc?"

"Wondered when you were going to show up," Adam said, drawing a circle in the air with his right hand, palm out.

"That ain't going to work. None of your fancy hocus-pocus is going to work."

"Night vision goggles in a lighted room? Not too swift," Brett said, stepping toward the masked intruders. He was immediately broadsided with the butt of an AR-15. He fell to the floor.

"The camouflage is not necessary. I know who you are. What do you want?" Adam said.

"Yeah, we know who you are. You bastards. Still think you're in the Seals with all that shit you're wearing?" Running-water said, moving his hand slowly to his backside.

"I wouldn't do that," Dutch said, jabbing a modified AR-15 at Running-water. "I'll ask just once more. Where are the whore and the doc?"

"There's no whore here and Doctor Bach is in the village," Adam said, walking closer to the massive fireplace.

"Nobody said you could move," Will Rexford said.

A shrill scream filled the air; uncontrollable sobbing followed it. The sound of gunfire had brought Julie into the main house. Finding Samuel slumped on the floor of the entryway she thought the worst. That moment of distraction was all Adam needed. He slung the fireplace poker across the room. Dutch opened his mouth in disbelief as the poker pierced his throat, shoving his microphone back until it exited at the back of his head.

Will Rexford cried out in pain. A knife thrown by Isha struck him just under the collarbone. Yanking out the knife, he whirled to open fire. Multiple shots from Running-water's Glock ripped off his face. The AR-15 clattered on the marble floor. The assassins' blood pooled around their lifeless bodies. Adam heard Julie's sobs and he went to her and her stricken husband.

"Oh, Adam. I think he's dead. I can't lose him! I just can't!" Julie whispered, clutching Adam's arm. Her black mascara and her twisted mouth open in horrified fear presented a near macabre image of Edvard Munch's *The Scream.*

Adam placed his hands over Samuel's body, moving them slowly around until they found their own place. Hovering over Samuel's head, Adam's hands showed a blue aura. He gently applied pressure. His hands changed to bright red as the heat built; their skin cracked and began to bleed.

Feeling someone's arm around him, Adam looked up. It was Running-water. Gently, he began to pat Adam's bleeding hands with a damp cloth. Flashes of blue light sparked between them. Jerking his hands, back, startled Running-water wasn't sure what was happening. Then he remembered their experience on the mountain. He placed his hands on top of Adam's, and the flashing blue light grew brighter. This time there were no drums beating; two hearts beat in synchronization. Adam and Running-water's eyes locked. Both understood. No more animosity. Samuel groaned, opened his eyes, and sputtered, "Adam, I'm sorry."

"Nothing to worry about, my friend. Just relax. You've had quite a blow to your head. Get up very slowly," Adam said, as Running-water slid his hands and arms under Samuel, ready to help him get up.

"Man! I never thought they'd go this far," Running-water said. "Seems too radical just because I fired Dutch. You know something I don't?"

"Nothing specific. That's why it is important for me to do this thing with Christine. That may not happen now. But first, call the sheriff. I'll check on our guests."

Whether it was the use of our or Adam's tone that struck him. Whichever it was, it signaled that the world was right between them. "Wonder if Adam suspected we were real brothers. How can we possibly be twins," Running-water thought?

128

CHAPTER FIFTEEN

Christine Lilith Conduit had her bag. She had decided she would have nothing more to do with Adam or his group. The smell of cordite, the coppery smell of blood, the grotesqueness of it all sickened her. They wouldn't dare to force me to stay. "No, I don't think so," she thought. She clutched her laptop close to her breasts. It was her life. She was to be in Houston the day-after-tomorrow. Still clutching her laptop to her bosom, she reached in her bag and pulled out a cell phone. She decided to call her hotel and see if she could have her room earlier. The sooner I get out of here the better. Registration for the conference on Psycho-neuropathology was not a problem. She was, after all, the keynote speaker. She'd already signed up for several of the sub-sessions: Neural Basis for Consciousness, Space-Time Relationship, and Parapsychology. This whole business here sickens. Feeling someone watching her, she gave a little shudder.

Turning from the large window, she saw Esaugetuh looking at her. "Let him say whatever he wants. I'm not changing my mind. I'm out of here!"

"I have no such intention," Esaugetuh said, walking over to her.

She forgot to keep her mind clear. Reading people's thoughts was how he knew she had wanted him to bed her down. A smile appeared at the corner of her lips as she remembered their tryst twenty years ago. Quickly, she cleared her mind of those thoughts.

"I'm glad you're not going to try to change my mind. It wouldn't do you any good. Right now all I want is to get out of here as fast as I can," Christine said.

"As soon as we know the condition of everyone, I'll see that you are driven to the airport," Esaugetuh said.

Daphne walked in, composed and stunningly beautiful. Her black hair framed her face, accenting her doe eyes. She was a stark contrast to the bloodied room. "This must be a horrid experience for you. Because there have been so many attempts on Adam's life we probably seem quite callous. Actually, we are not. Hopefully, you won't hold this mess against us."

"Of course not. It's just— well, I'd just like to get out of here," Christine said.

"I'm sorry things didn't work out. I agree with you about getting out of here. Come up to my apartment and join the four of us for a drink," she said nodding toward Isha, Patricia, and Genevieve. Come, join us," Daphne said, putting her arm around Christine.

Grateful for a chance to escape the horror the women gladly accepted Daphne's invitation. On their way to the elevator, Daphne asked Isha to go and get Julie. On their way to the third-floor Daphne decided there would be no aged brandy for this group. Martinis were called for. She and Isha soon had a tray of snacks fit for any queen: Russian caviar, hardboiled pheasant eggs, imported cheeses,

130

fruit salsas, toasted bread, and assorted chocolate truffles. Daphne made the martinis extra dry and then gently splashed them over ice in a crystal pitcher. A fire in the massive fireplace nearly completed the carefully orchestrated setting. Daphne put a CD in a player. The songs by the Native Flute Ensemble filled the room. She thought their Spirit Seekers Ceremony was appropriate. Julie, a recovering alcoholic, had a lemon splash.

Once they had their drinks, Daphne excused herself and went to her sons. She returned with them. Quietly, she set them upon the floor, directly in front of Christine Lilith Conduit. "I'd like you to meet my sons," Daphne said. "In the order of their births they are Mahpee, meaning the sky, next Mhkah, which means earth, next is Miri, which means water, and then Paytah whose name means fire. Are they not beautiful?"

Awed by the light-blue glow surrounding each, Christine managed to say, "Yes. Beautiful. They have their father's eyes." Once again, she felt the pang in her being; that old longing. She shook her head to clear the thought.

"Isha, who is my sister-in-law, has a set of twin boys. Older than my quads," Daphne said. Turning to Isha, she continued, "Why don't you go and get them so Christine and Genevieve can meet them?"

"How do you feel about not being Running-water's twin?" Christine said, deliberately changing the subject from children.

The question caught Daphne off guard. She had not considered it. She was at a loss for words. Remembering the time, she had seen Running-water

131

naked, her face reddened. His sensuousness as he handled his private parts aroused her, and she had wanted him. She had been hiding in the shrubbery as he climbed out of their swimming pool. She remembered the shame she had felt in lusting for her brother. Realizing that Christine was a spirit guide, Daphne quickly cleared her mind of those thoughts.

"Actually, I've not had time to consider it. Having been raised as brother and sister I doubt there will be any significant change in our relationship."

Isha and her twin boys arrived. She placed them in the semi-circle in front of Christine Lilith Conduit and Genevieve Van Batten. Both women had expected them to crawl around, but they didn't. They sat, fixated on Christine. A lifetime passed. The hypnotic moment broke with Adam's arrival. The quads, as well as the twins, radiated a pale blue aura; their skin tone had a bluish cast to it. Christine caught the physical change, but before she could ask about it, Adam said, "I've arranged for your return to Denver. My helicopter is ready to fly you to Bellingham. I have ordered that my new jet be made ready."

"A new jet?" Daphne said, surprised by her husband's nonchalant announcement.

"Yes, a Cessna Citation X. It flies just under the speed of sound. Much faster than the other one. The accommodations are more spacious and comfortable," Adam replied. He turned to Christine, bent down, took her hands, and kissed her on the check. "I appreciate your coming out here, and I accept your reluctance to help bilocate me. Hopefully, this additional five thousand will help make the situation less disagreeable."

"I hope you really do understand. I really do. The money is not necessary. I do have a favor to ask if you can arrange it. I don't want to go back to Denver. I'm supposed to be in Houston tomorrow to deliver a speech. Could you arrange for me to fly there?"

"No problem. I'll ask Brett to change the flight plan."

A phone buzzed. It was Running-water calling to tell them the sheriff had arrived. Adam returned to the first floor.

CHAPTER SIXTEEN

The all too familiar yellow tape hung around the front portico and across the sliding doors to the great room. Being careful not to disturb the bodies, forensics went to work gathering evidence. While they waited for the coroner to arrive, the sheriff and his deputies began interviewing the witnesses. At Adam's request, Christine Lilith Conduit was first and then Brett Montana. That would allow them to expedite their flight to Bellingham. Both agreed to be available for further questions or if there was an inquest. Within minutes after their statements, the chopper lifted off and was soon out of sight.

They flew along the I-5 corridor to Bellingham. Too absorbed in her own thoughts, Christine didn't notice the beauty of the area. Upon landing, Brett filed a new flight plan to Houston rather than Denver. They boarded an ATV to shuttle them out to Adam's private hanger; there they discovered that the new Cessna Citation X had not been delivered. On their way, back to the main terminal Brett called Adam and brought him up to speed.

Inside, Christine bought a ticket on a commuter flight to SeaTac International where she would make a connection to Houston. As she exited the terminal to board her plane, she waved good-bye. Brett canceled the flight plan, returned to the chopper, and took off for the Monastery. He breathed a sigh of relief, glad that he didn't have to make the flight to Houston. Hope Adam decides to pick up another pilot and navigator.

Brett noticed two EMH vehicles parked in front of the mansion as he brought the chopper in for a landing. Samuel was waiting for him at the helipad. As they zoomed along on the ATV Samuel said, "Did you have any indication that Dutch and Will would try to murder Adam and Running-water? Jesus! I just can't imagine what got into them."

"None. Man! I never thought Dutch would be that big a sore head. Adam paid us both very well. So it shouldn't have been over money. Go figure," Brett replied.

"Makes you wonder what they wanted," Samuel said.

"Whatever it was, they must've wanted it really bad. Sure beats the hell out of me," Brett said. "Guess they didn't have any love for you either. You okay?"

"Couple sore ribs and a lump on the head. I'm no worse for the wear," Samuel said. Clearing his throat, Samuel continued, "That Will Rexford was sure an odd one, don't you think? And Dutch knew an awful lot about his physical being."

"What you driving at?" Brett asked. The ATV hit a bump, nearly spilling them.

"Well, I think they were gay," Samuel said.

"You homophobic?" Brett said as he piled out as Samuel pulled the ATV to a stop in front of the Monastery.

"Hell no. You live on the street as I did you learn tolerance. I just don't see the need for them to pretend. I'm sure it wouldn't make any difference to Adam. Weren't you surprised?"

135

"I didn't know Will Rexford existed. Dutch never mentioned him in all the time we were in the SEALS together. I think what you say is true. I suspect the militaries 'don't ask; don't tell' policy had something to do with their discretion."

"Yeah. I guess you're right," Samuel said as he punched in the code to open the front door.

Once inside, they stopped and watched the coroner as he supervised the bagging of the bodies. Two deputies remained in the great room. The sheriff was not present. Assuming he was at Adam's apartment, they headed to the elevator. Daphne let them in. Everyone glued to the large-screen television, listened to 'breaking news.'

A commuter plane from Bellingham crashed in the Sound. Details were still sketchy, but apparently, the small commuter jet had flown out over Deception Pass area and had plunged into the water. There had no distress call from the plane. Because of the whirlpools in that area, the officials didn't expect to find any survivors.

Brett was stunned.

"Did they say what plane it was?" Brett said.

"You heard everything we did," Adam said, "had fifteen people on board including the captain and a copilot.

"Christine Lilith Conduit was on that plane!" Brett said. His voice quivered.

"You're sure?" Adam said.

"Yes. She waved to me as she boarded the plane."

"Damn! I was sure she would change her mind and return after her conference. Any change of our

136

finding out who is really behind these new attacks on us is gone." Adam said his disappointment clear.

Adam was about to say something more but instead got real quiet. He didn't move as he listened and then looking at the six children still on the floor, a broad smile stretched across his handsome face. His azure blue eyes brightened. The boys were radiating blue flashes of light. He felt their vibrations and understood. Kneeling in front of them, he gently laid his hand on each boy's head and said, "Thank you."

Then as if nothing had transpired, Isha and Running-water's twins went about their play, and the quads began to crawl around.

Daphne looked at her husband. The death of Christine Lilith Conduit brought into focus all the other deaths of people associated with her husband. The continual increase in that number frightened her. Not just those who made a direct assault upon their lives but also those who died by association. She wondered how many, having never asked him about it. She was sure he knew.

"What is it?" Daphne asked.

"All is not lost," Adam replied.

The sheriff was completing his interviews, the last being Genevieve Van Batten. She was in a talkative mood.

"In the old days," she said, "I would have shot those ruffians myself. The nerve of them, busting in here."

"Yes, ma'am I'm sure you would have." Turning to Adam, he said, "I'm done here. You may be deposed, but I can't see any issues at the moment. You plan on being around?"

"Yes, I'll be here. How soon can I get the room cleaned and sanitized?"

"I'll check with the people downstairs." Addressing Running-water, the sheriff continued, "You want to go down with me? Perhaps you will go over a few last details with me."

On the elevator, the sheriff looking perplexed said, "The word is getting around that this place is nothing but a slaughterhouse. Any chance of your friend moving on?"

"Adam is my twin brother. We're not moving anymore. We'd hoped that Christine Lilith Conduit would have been able to help us find out who is been trying to kill us. Whoever it is has brought the battle into our home. We stay, and we fight! What would you have us do, sheriff?" Running-water said.

"I see your point."

"He may see my point, but he sure as hell didn't offer any suggestions," Running-water thought.

The elevator came to a halt at the first floor.

One of the myriads of issues that bothered Running-water was the whereabouts of Dr. Allan Bach. Upon their return from their near-disastrous trip from The Mittens, Dr. Bach was nowhere around. He did not answer his pager or his cell phone. It had surprised Running-water that Bach had not flown out to The Mittens to care personally for Adam.

"Sheriff—, before you leave, would you mind coming with me to check on one of our guests, Dr. Allan Bach. He's missing. Perhaps you can spot something in his rooms that I've overlooked. He bed doesn't look like it has been slept in," Running-water said.

The sheriff agreed. They went to Dr. Bach's three-room apartment in the mansion. None of his clothes seemed to be missing; no personal toiletries were missing. His medical bag sat on the floor next to his desk. The laptop was still on the desk. Nothing seemed out of place.

"What about his car?"

"He didn't have one," Running-water said. "All our vehicles are accounted for."

"Could someone have driven him into the village or had someone come out and pick him up?"

"None of us drove him into the village and according to our security tapes, no one picked him up. There is no record of his physical presence on any of the tapes. He just vanished," Running-water said.

"People just don't vanish. Well, maybe around here it's possible," the sheriff said.

"What the hell do you mean by that?" Running-water said.

"Things, many of them not so normal, have gone on here. Take the number of deaths, for example. None of them have been because of natural causes."

"And none of those have been deliberate on our part. Remember, sheriff, the assaults have been against us. And we do have the right to defend ourselves," Running-water said.

"Uh-huh. What about those two tonight? Adam said one was his pilot, and the other was supposed to be an agent for Homeland Security. What the hell was a Homeland Security type doing here? You got some explaining to do, and I want straight answers."

"And so would I. Believe me so would I," Running-water said.

They continued their search of the buildings. No trace of Dr. Bach. The sheriff decided to delay any further searching until morning. The floodlights left too many shadowy areas, creating false hiding places.

"You got a picture of this Dr. Bach? Would help if you had one. You'll have to file a missing person's report. Get some fliers printed up and placed at various places down in the village."

"Consider it done. How about a reward for information leading to finding him?" Running-water said.

"Won't hurt," the sheriff replied.

"How about fifty thousand dollars?"

"Whew! You really want this guy?"

"Yeah. He's our family doctor."

CHAPTER SEVENTEEN

Morning fog surrounded the mountain top monastery. Trees and shrubs dripping from the intense moisture became grotesque monsters in the hazed illumination created by the many floodlights around the main grounds of the old mansion. By all accounts, it would be noon before the fog burned off. Today Adam decided to have a community breakfast, the first gathering since his return from the desert. Besides the six children, there were eleven adults. Daphne watched him as he piled platters full with eggs, bacon, and ham. These, served up from warming ovens complimented stacks of buckwheat pancakes. Elegant crystal bowls filled with fresh fruit compote and pitchers of maple syrup served as willing toppers for the cakes.

Jedediah Woods folded his hands, bowed his head, and said, "Unto thee."

Those two words brought back a flood of memories for Adam as well as Running-water. They also added to the bits of information confirming that this man who uttered them was indeed Jedediah Woods, the biological grandfather of Daphne.

"You are so much like your grandmother, my beloved Marie Copa. All the times we had made love, I never knew she had a twin sister. I never knew they were both having sex with me, and I never knew I had a son. I have to admit I feel I'm not only one who has been duped," Jedediah said.

"Not duped, my old friend. All will be revealed in due time," Esaugetuh said.

"Whatever. Anyway, mighty fine breakfast, Adam. I see you haven't lost your touch. Speaking of touch, don't suppose you could do a healing session on my old back?"

Running-water sucked in his breath. Esaugetuh looked at Adam; eyes squinted in an effort to read his son's reactions. No one mentioned Adam's healing abilities since his return from the desert. They wondered about the unspoken—had Adam's ability to heal returned? Or had the She-Devil, Moon-Woman taken that away from him? Had that been her revenge?

Jedediah waited.

Before Adam could respond, the shrill sound of the buzzer at the main gate sounded.

Samuel excused himself and went to the control center. Sheriff Bolton and two deputies wanted entrance to the compound. Before admitting them, he called in the six Dobermans, something he had forgotten to do when he first got up. He'd been forgetting little things lately. He blamed the punch to his head. He pushed the button to allow the huge iron gate to slide open. He watched as the sheriff's car passed through. He pushed the button again and watched the gate close behind the slow-moving sheriff's car. It would be a few minutes before they reached the front portico.

As he waited for the sheriff, Samuel wistfully remembered the days at Karuna House, the Toronto mansion where The Brothers lived. The group breakfast brought back memories of past group gatherings. At the old Victorian mansion, The Brothers, Adam, and Running-water had their meals together. During the meal, each had the opportunity to contribute something to the conversation. He thought of the meditation sessions and particularly the time Charles had collapsed. Adam stopped the bleeding caused by Charles' self-castration. And that led him to think of Joseph and the horror he caused. He shuddered.

The noise of the sheriff's car brought him back to reality.

He picked up his Uzi and headed out the door. Before descending the steps of the portico he stopped, looked around."No one's going to blindside me again. What an embarrassment," he thought.

Samuel ushered the sheriff into a waiting room, leaving the two deputies and their cadaver sniffing dogs outside. Samuel buzzed Running-water on the intercom and then sat down outside the waiting room door, his back against the opposite wall.

"No, sir! No one's going to clobber me again. Least not from behind."

The sheriff, his deputies, and their dogs would join Running-water and Adam in a search of the hundred-acre compound. The five men fanned out with the dogs in the lead. Midday brought no signs of the missing Dr. Bach. Samuel and Brett joined the searchers. Late afternoon brought the group to the edge of the granite cliff.

"Hold it," Sheriff Bolton said.

"What? Running-water asked.

"It's my guess your missing man is down there. See those scuff marks and a couple of broken branches on that evergreen. Someone or something has gone off the edge.

"Brett, bring up one of the choppers and floodlight that whole area. Get in as close as you can," Adam said.

Within minutes, Brett was airborne. He climbed and then turned the chopper around so that he faced the downside of the steep cliff. Double lights from the chopper flooded the side of the cliff. It was sheer; no ledges. It looked like someone had taken a giant knife and sliced it straight down.

"If Bach went over he's got to be at the bottom. Nothing there for him to get hung up on," Brett thought.

Brett turned on his mike.

"I'm going lower down and come in toward the base. If he's down there that's where he's got to be."

He took his time scanning the area with binoculars. Something shiny caught his attention. He came back to it. He hovered there. Focused. "Yes. Hot dog! Three flashes in quick succession."

"I found him. He's alive," Brett shouted into his phone. "The terrain is overgrown brush. Too risky to land. I'm coming back to the pad."

Back at the monastery, Brett gathered up a couple of blankets, a first-aid kit, flashlight, box of matches, and plastic bottles of water. He wrapped all of this in bubble wrap and placed it in a canvas bag. He attached a long rope to the bag, slung it on the chopper, and took off. As soon as he was over the area, he switched on the chopper's floodlights. He waited. He saw it; the flash. He tossed the bag out the door; holding onto the rope. He felt the jerk and released the rope. Bach had his care package.

Dr. Bach gulped down one bottle of precious water. Using a second bottle, he washed the dried blood from his leg. The femur was so badly broken that a two-inch section of the bone struck out through the skin. Had the break gone a bit the other way it would have severed an artery. He wished he had a self-retaining nail kit, but since he didn't, he tried to bring the broken pieces back together by using his belt and part of his shirtsleeve. Excruciating pain shot through his leg. He fell back; unconscious. When he came to, he realized he was feverish, a sign of infection.

They had better get here soon. If they don't—.

He tried to sit up. He was sweating profusely. He lay back down. Panting from the effort. On the third attempt, he was upright. Bracing himself with one arm, he leaned over and began gathering leaves and twigs that were in reach. He struck a match and quickly blew it out.

"That's a stupid thing to do. They won't be searching for me in the dark. A whirring thumping penetrated his fevered mind. It can't be. I must be hearing things," he thought.

The sound grew louder. Blinding lights flicked on and off.

What the hell are they trying to tell me? Light! Of course. Light the damn fire. Once the fire caught and Brett saw it, he flicked the chopper's lights on and off a couple more times.

In his excitement, Bach tried to get up to wave. He screamed. A thousand needles jabbed into him

145

all at once. His vision blurred. Dizziness swarmed over him. Fighting to remain conscious, he began to yell, "The bear went over the mountain to see what he could see."

Rumbling in the low brush silenced him. "Shit. A bear? Now what?"

He saw lights. Hallucination. Fever. Delirium.

Muffled voices light-years away penetrated his fogged brain. The light hurt his eyes as he tried to focus. A huge figure stood over him. No Two figures.

"Well it's about time, sleeping beauty," Adam said.

"Yeah. Man, when you're out, you are really out," Running-water said.

"The doctors tell me you are going to be fine. They put some kind of a removable screw in your leg," Adam said. "You remember anything about how you got down at the bottom of the cliff?"

Alan Bach didn't hear him. He was in a drugged asleep.

"You still want me to post a deputy? It seems a bit unusual. However, if you got a reason to believe his fall wasn't an accident—,"

"Yes. Put a deputy at his door. There was an attempt on our lives. Mass execution was certainly the plan and Dr. Bach is a member of my household. Tomorrow I'd like you to join me and revisit the top of the cliff. Double-check to make sure nothing has been missed."

Once he had a deputy in place, Sheriff Bolton left.

Speaking to Running-water Adam said, "I will do a healing on Alan. Close the door."

Adam pulled the blanket and sheet from Alan's body. He placed his hands just above the broken leg and began a low-pitched hum. Slowly, it built until the sound filled the hospital room. Adam's hands were bright red and once again, the blue aura engulfed him. He was nearly transparent. Running-water felt the vibrations warming his body, and a renewed sense of well-being washed over him. "Great. Adam's got his healing powers back," he thought.

"And so they are, my brother; at least for now. I want to try something else before we leave. I want to try a brain scan. Perhaps I can still get an image of what happened. Alan may not remember what happened, but the images may still be present. I'll need a good fifteen minutes without interruption. Tell the deputy to allow no one into the room; not even the medical staff."

Running-water opened the door and spoke to the guard.

Adam sat down on the floor and began to meditate. Running-water watched as Adam's breathing slowed. A pale blue glow radiated around Adam. It gathered itself into a thin stream of blue light, not unlike a laser beam. Running-water watched the small undulations in the beam as it stretched out from Adam and settled around Dr. Bach's heart. There it brightened and grew larger. The beam hesitated for a moment testing the life force and then it slowly flowed up to his head. It gradually formed a halo around his head, came down the ridge of his nose, and disappeared into his slightly open mouth. A gasp, nearly inaudible escaped from Alan's parted lips. His head jerked and then was still.

Adam stood up; looked at Running-water, and sent him a telepathic message that there should be no oral communication between them. Without speaking, they left Dr. Bach's room, spoke briefly to the deputy, and took the elevator to the first floor. In the parking lot, they stopped, looked around, and then began to laugh. They laughed until tears rolled down their faces. There was no car for them to go home in. They had come in the ambulance. Once they stopped their laughing, they noticed a black stretch limo in the parking lot, lights on, and motor running.

"Samuel," Adam said.

On the road back to the Monastery, Adam told Running-water that he had learned that someone hit Alan Bach from behind and threw him over the cliff.

"There should be some indication where the attack occurred. Something should be there. We've just overlooked it."

"You figure it was Dutch and Will?" Running-water said. "That's a stupid question. Of course, you don't. Otherwise, you wouldn't have had a deputy posted at Alan's hospital room. Who? Mind filling me in?"

Adam pushed the intercom and spoke to Samuel. "How did Dutch and Will get to the Monastery? We didn't find any vehicle."

"No car. They were at the gate on foot. Like the idiot I am, I brought them up to the house in my ATV. As I got out, one of them hit me, knocking me to the ground. The other one, that bastard Will, kicked me twice. I tried to get up. Then, he slammed the butt of a gun to my head."

"Someone brought them to the entrance. I don't believe they hiked up there from the town. Not with all the weapons, they had with them. That someone may still be on the grounds. Notify Brett and have him move everyone into safe rooms," Adam said.

"It can't be Moon-Woman can it? She is dead, isn't she?" Running-water said.

"She is no more."

"Dutch and Will are dead. Who then?"

"That, my brother, is what we are going to find out.

CHAPTER EIGHTEEN

Adam called a group meeting in the large reception room of the old monastery. Located on the first floor, and just to the left of the main entrance, it remained a stark reminder of the horror it had witnessed. He decided to have everyone meet there to punctuate the serious nature of their safety. Bullet holes remained, and one chair still had bloodstains. Others were already there, watching and listening. Formless they moved about the old Monastery.

They were aware of the other pair of watchful eyes—those belonging to the human female with the camera. She still lived. They had not come to a decision about her. For now, Patricia Livingston would be allowed to live.

They knew the shaman's powers were increasing. He nearly caught them once; a fleeting shadow just as had the woman with the camera. They had to be more careful. To reveal themselves ahead of the scheduled time would not be tolerated. They hid themselves by taking on the shape of trees, shrubs, or flowers. All too well they understood the implications of the butterfly that flapped its wings.

Once the members of the compound assembled, Adam addressed the group.

"Alan was thrown over that cliff. Whoever is responsible may still be on the grounds. Everyone needs to be alert. Always go about in pairs. Patricia, you and Brett better move into the main house. Fewer problems if we are not scattered about. The women and children are never to be out without one of us being with you."

"I think we should set up a security watch. I'll take the first, Samuel you take the second and Adam you take the third," Running-water said.

"Wait a minute. What about me?" Brett said.

"No slight intended. You take the third watch and Adam you take the last. Agreed?"

"Remember there were those shadows on my video. I'm sure they were much more than the mere play of light through the trees," Patricia Livingston said.

"I remember, but I don't think those shadows, whatever they are, are responsible for the attack on Alan Bach."

Ah, she not only has eyes but a memory. She needs to be carefully watched.

With the morning's arrival, Adam's tension eased somewhat. However, he felt that their renewed search of the grounds, like the videos of Patricia Livingston, would reveal nothing new. He let his mind examine the possibility that the man now identified as Jedediah Woods was somehow still under the influence of Moon-Woman. To disquiet these thoughts Adam decided to test the old man one more time. If he passed the test, he would be free to go wherever he wished, even back to the log cabin in Pennsylvania.

"Jedediah, come walk with me," Adam said

Walking slowly they took in the fresh robust smell of the tall cedars, the more refined smell of hemlock, and the sweet smell of firs that populated the Monastery's grounds; all warm and inviting

Adam stopped, bent over, and using his hand to sweep away some of the pine needles, scooped up a handful of the warm earth. He held it in his hand for a moment, smelled it, and then let it filter through his fingers back to the ground. Its smell, the feel of pine needles underfoot, and the quietness massaged his soul. For a time, they continued their walk in silence; a silence that was broken by an occasional flutter of wings.

He stopped their walk, turned to the old man and looked directly at him.

"You miss it?"

"Man should never tire of that which nourishes him. It would be nice to plant again," Jedediah said.

"You never did explain why you didn't display your degrees on the walls of your cabin."

"Damn! You are stubborn. I told you they had no value to me. I don't need pieces of paper to remind me of my accomplishments or lack thereof. I know what I have done or not done. I thought you understood you didn't need pieces of paper or token awards to prove your worth," Jedediah grumbled. "What's really sticking in your craw?"

"Fair enough question. I haven't been sure you are who I think you are. Your presence in the desert is too coincidental. Just how did you get into the desert?"

"To quote a young smart-passed friend of mine, 'I am that I am!'"

"And that you are."

"I don't exactly know how I got into The Mittens. I'm sure I didn't walk there. I have to admit that I am disappointed that Running-water is

152

not my grandson. I'd always fancied a son and a grandson. That Daphne, your wife, is a spitting image of the only woman I ever loved. It will be interesting to see how Esaugetuh explains your real relationship to Running-water. Aren't you the least bit curious?" Jedediah said.

A movement to his left caught Adam's attention. He stopped. A shadow seemed to float along the lower branches of the trees. Not sure, if he saw someone, or if it was a leaf falling, or the sun playing games, teasing him, Adam took his time looking around. His eyes searched the woods. He listened for sounds. There were none. No birds chirping, squirrels chattering. None of the usual forested sounds. Those that lived in the woods surrounding the Monastery had adjusted to the presence of humans once more living in their space. With the appearance of the shadow, all became dead quiet. No gentle morning breeze moved a branch. There should have been a breeze.

He quieted his breathing. Whispering? He strained to hear. He drew a wide circle with his palm, and the area took on a macroscopic appearance. He scanned the area. No one. Closing his hand and opening it again, cleared the vision.

The only thing he heard was Jedediah wheezing. He took him by the arm and hurried along the path back to the Monastery.

CHAPTER NINETEEN

They began another search of the compound. A thorough search of the outbuildings revealed nothing. They revealed nothing. Adam made a search of the vehicles and of the two helicopters. And like the others, he found nothing. Inside, Daphne, Julie, and Isha made a search of every nook and cranny in the mansion. Genevieve Van Batten played grandmother to the twins and the quads. Running-water busied himself checking through all of Adam's financial accounts. He wanted to see if there had been any unusual activity. Adam stopped at the office.

"When are you going to fill me in?" Running-water said.

"Have you made a complete electronic sweep of all the buildings, especially our house?" Adam said.

Running-water seethed over having his question ignored. Adam's use of 'our' was generally a powerful palliative. But not this time. Running-water was not having any of it.

"You didn't tell me you wanted a sweep of *our* house. We can go to one of *our* safe rooms, and you can tell me who it is you suspect is behind the attempts on *our* lives. And damn it, Adam; don't give me this 'all in good time my brother' bullshit. I'm not buying it."

"Would you, of all people, being the attorney you are, have me accuse someone before I had the facts?" Adam said, looking directly at Running-water.

154

"I'm not just anybody. I'm your goddamn twin brother, for Christ's sake. I'm your attorney. You have heard of attorney-client confidentially?" It was the first time he had actually verbalized an acknowledgment that they were biological twins.

"Who would benefit from my death?" Adam said.

"What? Oh, shit! Don't tell me you suspect me?"

"Of course not. Don't get overly dramatic. You drew up our wills, community property agreements, living wills, power of attorneys. What happens if both of us and our families are dead?"

"The whole-she-bang goes into a trust."

"And who controls that trust?" Adam said.

"What? I don't believe it. No way! That's absolutely ridiculous." Running-water said.

"Now you know why I want to be absolutely sure."

"By the way, have you seen Samuel and Brett?" Running-water asked.

"Yes. I asked them to go down to the base of the cliff and do a search."

***

Adam asked Patricia Livingston to go with Samuel and Brett. She would film the area for later viewing. While packing her cameras she remembered she had to notify her studio at Toronto that she would not be returning. She had been thinking about how to go about doing that for some time.

155

"Maybe I'll just announce it in my last show. I'm doing a video now to send up. Make that one the last. Why not? I can just see the producer's mouth pop open," she mused.

She caught the news on the CBC a couple of times. She closely watched her replacement. "I hate to admit it, but she does a good job." She realized she was fondling her camera, petting and stoking it. Just for an instant, she wondered if she was making a mistake.

"No. No mistake this time."

She jammed the camera into her backpack, grabbed a bottle of water and joined Samuel and Brett in the SUV.

"Expecting trouble?" Patricia Livingston said, noting that both men were heavily armed.

"Just being cautious," Brett replied.

The SUV snaked its way down the long winding road to the main gate. Patricia looked back. The two 'old ones again stationed themselves on the roof of the Monastery. Out of habit, she took a couple of pictures.

She hadn't wanted to leave her writing, but as she looked about, she was grateful for the chance to get off the mountain.

"Maybe we can have lunch in the village," she thought.

Tears began to flow. She missed the city, her high-rise condo, and yes, the nervous energy before a broadcast.

"I never imagined living my life on top of a mountain. And of all places in a monastery, like a cloistered nun. Hell, I even miss the one-nighters.

It's not that Brett isn't good in bed. Actually, he's damn terrific. It's the -- the excitement," she thought.

She wiped the tears with the back of her hand. She caught the flash of sunlight in the two-carat diamond on her finger. She smiled. "I am where I am supposed to be."

CHAPTER TWENTY

Adam was openly disappointed. The call from Brett that he, Samuel and Patricia Livingston had found no evidence that Dutch and Will had scaled the 400-foot cliff

He paced back and forth.

"I was sure that Alan Bach had seen them, and they had attacked him, throwing him over the cliff. If they didn't come up the cliff, how did they get here? Samuel let them in at the gate, drove them to the main house. If they didn't try to kill Alan, who did?"

He stopped pacing. Looked about. The room needed cleaning. It remained a bloody reminder of the deadly assault that had taken place. The beautiful mahogany sliding doors were in shambles, riddled by the barrage of bullets from Dutch's AK-14. Even the furniture did not escape.

"A real mess, wouldn't you say?" Adam said.

Running-water didn't respond. Like the room itself, he was in emotional disarray. Too much happened. The man whom he considered his best friend, his soul mate, had turned out to be his biological twin. The woman, whom he thought was his twin sister, wasn't. The woman whom he called mother wasn't. And now this man whom they sought as Adam's father is his father as well. Adam's murdered mother was his mother. And like the mahogany doors, Running-water's soul was riddled with holes, holes of doubt.

"Jesus. Everything I ever knew or believed has been shattered. Now what?"

Coming from a great distance, light-years away from where he was, Running-water vaguely heard Adam's voice. He blinked his eyes and shook his head to shatter the morose trance that held him. He looked at Adam, seeing him for the first time.

"You say something?" Running-water said.

"It was of no consequence. I've asked our father, Esaugetuh, The Master of Breath, to explain our relationship. He has agreed to do so after our evening meal. He wants to have everyone hear what he has to say. I agreed. Do you, my friend?"

The not so subtle shift from the usual 'my brother' to 'my friend' was noted.

"Your damn right I agree. I want him to explain his reasons for all the manipulation and subterfuge. Jesus Adam, doesn't it piss you off? You know, being used for some greater good or purpose without being consulted. Doesn't it make you angry that we have nearly lost our lives on several occasions? It sure as hell does me."

"Remember my friend, we were motivated in our search for the man whom we now know as our father. We launched into the puzzle, the mystery, and intrigue with the intent of solving it. Like two hungry wolves, we pursued our prey. We could have refused the challenge. We did not. It was our choice. You've got to admit it's been an adventure and then some, hasn't it?" Adam said

Running-water snapped to complete attention. The words 'my friend' and the emphasis on 'has been' grabbed him. He looked at Adam, searched

159

his azure blue eyes trying to get an indication at the true meaning behind the change in words.

"Are you saying we are done?"

Entering the room, Daphne announced, "Jedediah is ready to give the blessing. Come to the main dining room. Dinner is ready."

Running-water's unanswered question added to his gloominess. It spread, contagiously infecting the other diners. They ate in silence except for an occasional pass, this or that. Patricia Livingston credited the gloom to the lack of success in finding evidence linking the assault upon Dr. Bach to Dutch Masters and Will Rexford.

"I may have something on the video I took while we were at the base of the cliff. If you want, we can take a look at them later," Patricia Livingston said.

"Doubtful if anything is there," Adam replied.

"You never know. It's true the camera lens is sometimes unkind, even cruel, but it also is all-seeing. It picks up what we humans fail to register."

"Tomorrow, maybe. Tonight belongs to Esaugetuh. He has a story he wants to tell us," Adam said.

"Is this something I may record or is it off the record?" Patricia Livingston said. She was now used to asking for permission to record.

"For the record," Esaugetuh said. "I have to tell this my way. When I'm finished, I'll answer questions, but not until then. Agreed?" He looked up and down the table making sure there was agreement.

"Screw you old man. I don't want to hear any of your goddamned long stories. All I want to know is why you preferred Adam over me," Running-water blurted, getting up to leave.

"Sit down and clean up your mouth," Adam said.

"And who's going to make me, dear brother?"

Ignoring the sarcasm, Adam raided his right hand, drew a circle, and pushed its palm forward. The force slammed Running-water back into his chair, nearly toppling it. His eyes enlarged with disbelief.

"I am! And in *our* home, you will show respect."

There it is again—*our*. It's just a possessive pronoun. It has no significant meaning beyond possessiveness.

Running-water struggled to breathe. Red-faced and flushed with anger he tried to get up. The more he struggled the more difficult it was for him to breathe. Adam's extended right hand relentlessly held him there. Running-water went limp; his head fell forward.

"Please, Adam. For god's sake. Release him," Isha cried. "He's the father of my children."

Adam lowered his hand. Running-water stirred, straightened up in his chair. Tears streamed down his handsome face. He looked at Adam and whispered.

"Why?"

"Simple. I love you, my brother. And just as I do, you need answers to your questions. Had you left, you would not have those answers and there

161

would be no peace in your soul or in mine. I am as curious as you are. One more piece of our puzzle is about to be revealed. Do you really want to miss out on that? If you do, you are free to leave."

Running-water stood up. As he did, Adam stood and hugged his brother.

"I am that I am; you are that you are," Running-water whispered.

"And so we are," Adam replied. Turning to Esaugetuh, Adam said, "Begin your story, Old One."

CHAPTER TWENTY-ONE

"We are born," Esaugetuh began, "with certain innate abilities. I prefer to call them gifts of the Spirits. In my case, my gifts were those of the medicine man. I was the seventh of the seventh. My gifts as a healer revealed themselves at an early age at which time my father began to teach me.

Esaugetuh paused. He to his time looking at each person at the long table. He stopped at Running-water.

"You have already heard a couple of my early experiences, Running-water. I won't repeat them again. When I succeeded my father, my fame as a healer had grown throughout all the People. Gradually, as I gained experience, I realized I had other gifts. Unlike some other shaman, drugs were not necessary for me to go into Dreamtime."

Esaugetuh slid his chair back and stood up. Picked up his goblet and took a sip of wine. He cleared his throat and then continued.

"I had visions, and sometimes actually talked with the Spirits. During one of those times, I was told that I should seek to mate outside my tribe. In their wisdom, they told me that my bloodline was weakening. I systematically mated with several women from other tribes. None produced an heir."

"How was it you mated with a white woman; the woman whom you say is our mother and not Cornelia whom Daphne and I know as our mother?" Running-water said.

"How to go about finding a non-Indian woman was a mystery to me. Unlike the old traditions, I just couldn't go to a place and offer horses or blankets, or beads. I had done some healing with whites, especially those that lived in the outer areas. Anyway, a tribe in New York State sent for me. One of their young women, in labor, was unable to deliver her child. She belonged to a chief and he, like me, had no sons to connect him to eternity. Midwives were unable to relieve her suffering."

"What in the world did you do?" Daphne said.

"Well, I gave her some narcotic herbs and hypnotized her. When I was sure she was under, I reached into her womb. The child had turned around so I clasped it by its feet, held them together, and pulled the baby out."

Daphne looked at Adam and gave him a knowing wink. "So, she thought, son like the father." That brought a smile to her face. He reached over and gently touched her hand.

"What an unbelievable experience. A breached birth," Jedediah said. "Then what?"

"I stayed a few extra days to make sure she and her son were recovering. One day, while I was out for a long walk, I came upon a young white woman. Her horse threw her. She was unconscious. I'm a trembler, so I let my hands hover over her. They told me she had a brain injury. I wiped away some dried blood and placed both hands on her head. They began to vibrate as the healing took place."

"Uh-huh. I remember you gave a lecture on trembling," Jedediah said. "I think it was—,"

"She was absolutely beautiful. Long black hair surrounded the face of an angle. When she opened her eyes, they were breathtaking; doe eyes, deep black, and liquid. Her horse was nearby and I brought it to her, helped her into the saddle, and walked with her until we reached her father's house. She was sixteen, and I had found the love of my life."

Esaugetuh took a deep breath, sat back down. He looked at Genevieve Van Batten, patted her knee and gave her a wink. She understood. She was his love now. She touched his hand, gently squeezed it. She leaned over, kissed him on the cheek.

"It's okay. Tell them the whole story," she whispered.

"I remained in the area, hoping against hope to see her again. We met on the trail one day and after that, we secretly continued to meet. How we loved, our passion knew no boundary. Then one day, she told me she was pregnant. I was ecstatic; she dismayed. I went to her parents and asked them to allow me to marry her. Her father went ballistic; her mother became totally unraveled. They forbade us to see each other; threatening me with imprisonment. One Sunday while they were at church, she stood outside, waiting for them to finish speaking to the preacher. I grabbed her and fled back to my people. Believing she was a bad omen, they rejected her."

"Sounds like one of those romance novels I used to read. What happened next?" Julie said.

In her seventh month, I took her back to her parents. I had written to her father, offered him a large sum of money if he agreed to a pre-arranged marriage for his daughter with a white man. One of the white families I had helped with an illness had an eligible son. He agreed to marry your mother. As a wedding gift, I gave him one hundred thousand dollars and a promise that there would be an annual income of like amount until the child reached eighteen. One-half of that income went into a trust for my son. Like you Adam, I didn't know there was more than one child. I thought everything was fine. It wasn't."

"What happened?" Daphne said, leaning forward. She was just as curious as the rest about her parents.

"When it was revealed that twins were expected, the intended groom and his family balked. They were adamant. He would accept only one child. There was no history of twins in his family. Actually, they were concerned that one might not look like a white person. I convinced them to go ahead with the marriage. I arranged for them to go to New Mexico to be married and to stay there until sometime after the birthing."

Esaugetuh got up again from his chair, walked around the table, sipped a brandy handed to him by Adam. For a time, he stood looking out one of the expansive windows that graced the one side of the dining room. Despite his years, he was still a commanding figure, lean with pronounced muscularity. He was gathering his thoughts, searching for the right words to continue.

Running-water watched Esaugetuh, calculating his age. His eyes widened as he realized Esaugetuh must have been sixty years old when he and Adam were conceived. He wondered how such an old man could have had sperm strong enough to produce anything let alone twins.

Adam read Running-water's thoughts and sent him a telepathic answer.

He is a shaman, remember.

They both smirked, feigned a cough to cover it up. Their father not to be outdone said, "Believe me. I wonder how I could have done that myself. I've always credited it to the will of the Spirits."

Both Running-water and Adam had forgotten Esaugetuh was also a telepath and could tune into their thoughts. Color flushed their faces, embarrassed that they had been caught speculating about their sire's sex life.

"During my travels in the States," Esaugetuh continued, "I learned of a young woman, widowed by the war, who was expecting. I arranged for your mother to deliver at the same hospital. Once your mother birthed, I took one of you and placed you with Daphne's mother, arranged for the birth certificates to indicate twins born to one, a single to the other. I arranged for Adam's new parents to bring him to Canada. Because he was the first-born, I thought he was the one to succeed me. I provided for both of you, ensuring your education and general well-being. Once I was sure Adam was the one to replace me, I began his training. I even arranged for Running-water and Adam to meet. The rest, you pretty much know."

Esaugetuh drained his glass of brandy and then sat down. His shoulders seemed to cave in, and his

167

skin tone grayed. The recent battle with Moon-Woman, Adam's illness, and the struggle in the desert laid claim to him. He straightened, leaned over to Genevieve, took her hand, and kissed it.

"It's not that I favored one of you over the other, or I loved one of you less. I have and still do love you both, each in your own way. There has never been any intent on my part to slight you, Running-water. My Dreamtime revealed only one of you would be a shaman—that only one of you could be a shaman. If you recall, Adam, I told you there could only be one. Unfortunately, you interpreted that to mean you or me. I meant of the two of you. And that brings me to Cornelia. To this day, she does not know that you and Daphne are not twins and that you are not both her children. I made sure both of you were cared for by establishing Gordon Rapport, your uncle, as my attorney. I could keep tabs on you through him. Like, Cornelia, he does not know that Running-water is my son."

Running-water didn't accept what he heard. He remembered a letter addressed just to Adam in which Esaugetuh poured out his heart to 'his son.' His face burned. He struggled to compose himself. He took several deep breaths to calm himself. It didn't work.

"You never wrote me a letter telling me how sorry you were to have missed my growing into manhood. Not one word telling me you were proud of me. Nor did I receive any of your goddamn pearls of wisdom. How can you sit here and tell me in front of everyone, that you showed no favoritism? That you loved us equally? Just because you are old doesn't give you the right to lie. God knows there have been enough lies."

Isha went to her husband; their twins followed her. They climbed upon Running-water's lap. Isha bent down and softly said, "But you are loved."

"There was a letter to you. I wrote to both of you on the same day; the day of your sixteenth birthday. I was not aware you found the letter I wrote to Adam. There should have been an envelope addressed to you, Running-water. I don't understand why they weren't together," Esaugetuh said.

In spite of the hurt in the Esaugetuh's voice, Running-water was still not satisfied.

"Where did you put the letters?"

"In a drawer in a small medicine cabinet in my apartment over Cid's Bar. If you found one in the drawer, the other should have been with it."

"It wasn't. And another thing. You gave everything to Adam. Why didn't you divide it between us?" Running-water said.

"Ah, now the real question comes out. And I will give you an answer. I couldn't trust you with it. You had only one thing on your mind, having sex. Even though you got good marks all through your early schooling and in law school, you pursued only one ambition, getting laid. How could I possibly trust a huge sum of money to you? When I finally got you and Adam together it sobered you, brought you to maturity with specific responsibility— guarding his life. No one else could have done that, not even now. I mean no offense, Samuel. You've done an excellent job. In my letter to you, I told you

I had set up a special fund for you, with twenty-five million dollars in it. How much of that money do you still have?" Esaugetuh said.

"What? I'd sure like to know where the hell it is. I've never seen any such money. My uncle put me through law school, gave me a job, and looked after me, even brought an apartment in Albuquerque for my use. You sure as hell didn't. I told you no more lies, old man," Running-water said.

"Regardless of your feelings, I can prove I put that amount into an account for you, a living trust. My money bought the house for Cornelia; there was no large insurance from the military. I personally delivered the check to her. She thought I was from an insurance company. My money provided the funds for her to finish her education. A scholarship program set up just for her. I did watch you."

"Oh, sure you did. I never met you when I was young."

"You remember going to see the white buffalo right after it was born? You were seven years old. You pretended to be a teenager. Both you and Daphne were mature for your age."

"Well, yeah, I do remember. But I'm sure I was in my teens. Leastways, that's how I remember it. I also remember you. You made a real splash in the crowd that was there. Everyone stepped aside for you. Yeah, I remember wondering who you were."

And did something happen there?" Esaugetuh said.

"What do you mean, happen?"

"How did you respond when we met?" Esaugetuh said, ignoring the belligerency.

"I felt weird. Awkward, more likely. I felt like my body had been looked through."

"And it was. At that moment, I once again confirmed that you could not be a shaman. I'm tired. Perhaps tomorrow I'll answer your questions."

It was an effort for Esaugetuh to get out of his chair. Revealing all this tired him. He went to his room. Genevieve Van Batten followed him. The others sat in silence for a time; finally, those who had their own apartments left. Daphne gathered up her sons and put them to bed. When she returned Adam was gone.

CHAPTER TWENTY-TWO

Once Adam arrived on the first floor, he immediately went to the control center of the compound. Samuel was there doing his nightly check of the grounds.

"Samuel, I want to go to the hospital and check on Dr. Bach. Bring around the SUV. Check its gas and equipment. Notify me when you are at the front of the house."

"I'm on it," Samuel said.

The guard dogs immediately confronted him as he approached the garage. He spoke the necessary command, and they sat down. Samuel checked the SUV for armaments and then filled it with gas. He drove to the front of the building and notified Adam.

Adam walked down the steps of the portico. Samuel was standing by the car; its door open. Running-water dashed out the front door.

"You're not going anywhere without me. Sam, you drive. I may behave like an ass, but I'm not one. There needs to be some changes made and now is as good a time as any."

"Uh-huh. I found the old ones asleep on the roof. Sam needs some quality time off. Jedediah and our father should be enjoying their winter years, drift into Dreamtime, and enjoy their memories. And you, my brother?" Adam said.

"Isha misses her parents. I'm sure Daphne would like to see our mother—I mean her mother. It might be a good time to get them out of the house and take our sons with them."

"Isha's parents are retired, and school is not yet in session. Why not bring all of them here for a visit. If what I suspect is true, sending our families to New Mexico may actually put them in danger."

"Oh, man! What an idiot. Of course, they would be safer here."

"You said it. I didn't, " Adam said, laughing as he gave Running-water a cuff aside of the head.

"Do we need an excuse to get them here? Brett can fly out and get them. The new plane is at Bellingham. I did check that out."

"Do grandparents need an excuse to visit their grandchildren? I think not. However, we need to warn Cornelia not to reveal anything about her doings to anyone. You better have her phone checked to see if it has been bugged."

"No problem. The Old One really laid a trip on us tonight. I got a lot of answers. Don't misunderstand. They haven't made me feel any better. I still have a bunch of questions. A couple of big ones. To begin with, did you know I was your twin?" Running-water said.

"No. I knew there was a bond between us; one stronger than just being friends. I realized we were soul-mates; spiritually connected and accepted that as the reason for the stronger bond. How about you?"

"I had no idea. I just felt drawn to you much in the same way a magnet draws iron and a powerful magnet at that. I have another question."

"And that is?"

"Do you love me? I mean really love me and that your feelings are not just something arranged by our father?" Running-water said.

"I love you, my brother. And I hold you to your vow. This thing I am about to undertake is very dangerous. I need to know that you will hold the line."

"The line will be held. I want to take this trip with you. I want to see the bastard's face when he's confronted."

"Actually I'd like to avoid a confrontation right now. I need to get evidence that he's behind these attacks on us. I want to know if there is a connection between Moon-Woman and him. When we get back to the Monastery, we'll check that old medicine cabinet to see where your letter is. If mine was there, yours should be."

The SUV turned into the main parking lot of the hospital. Samuel pulled into a slot close to the entrance.

"You want me to come in with you or stay with the car?"

"Stay with the vehicle," Adam said.

"And Sam, stay alert," Running-water said.

Inside, a nurse informed them that they could not see Alan Bach. Unless they had other business, they should leave. Adam looked directly at her, fixed her gaze, and then moved his finger down her nose. He whispered something to her. No longer seeing them, she went about her business.

Dr. Bach was restless and moaning when Adam and Running-water entered his private room. At bedside, Adam quietly spoke Alan's name.

174

"I was dreaming. I didn't hear you come in. Thanks for coming by. What time is it, anyway?" Alan said.

"A little after midnight. Tell me about your dream," Adam said. "It might be helpful in finding out what happened to you."

"You remember leaving your apartment?" Running-water said.

"I think so---I decided to go for a walk. It was a nice evening. I needed to do some thinking. For some time, I had been trying to decide how to tell you that I wanted to go back to Toronto---to---to run the sanitarium, and to make a deal with you to let me buy it."

"The women will hate to see you go. Me too, but I do understand. The sanitarium is yours. You've more than earned it. Running-water will see to the necessary paperwork. About your dream." Adam said.

"I was outside. I'm not quite sure where, and I was being attacked by giant birds."

"Giant birds?" Running-water said.

"Yes. They kept dive-bombing me, forcing me to lay flat on the ground."

"Hmm. Did the ground have a particular smell to it?" Adam said.

"I don't know. I don't remember any smell. I do remember brushing pine needles and pine cones from under my face." Alan said.

"The pine cones. Were they big, small, long, round?" Adam said.

"Small round ones. Is this important?" Alan said.

"Maybe. Did the birds make any noise? Squawk?" Adam said.

"No. I don't think so. That's what was so strange. Just a swoosh sound. Oh, yes. I felt the air from their wings as they flew over me."

"You said birds. How many?" Running-water said.

"Two."

How did your dream end?" Adam said.

"I tried getting up, but one of them struck me with its feet.

"Uh-huh. Do you remember being picked up?" Adam said.

"Off the ground?" Alan said.

"No. Up in the air. By one of the birds."

"I'm not sure. I really don't remember." Alan said.

Turning to Running-water, Adam said, "What flies, makes very little sound other than swoosh as it passes by?"

"Hang gliders. I'll be damned. They used hang gliders with their motors cut off as they approached the Monastery. But how'd they get out on the road at the gate for Samuel to let them in?" Running-water said.

"Good question. Alan has just told us what happened to him. Alan, when you are well enough I'll have Brett fly you back to Toronto. We'll check you again later in the day."

Out in the corridor, Adam stopped and spoke to the deputy on duty. He then called Sheriff Bolton, told him about the gliders, and suggested the deputy was no longer needed. He and Running-water went to the parking lot. Samuel brought up the SUV. On their way south on I-5 Adam was absorbed in his own thoughts. He didn't notice that the moon was high and was bathing everything in a slivery afterglow. Traffic was still sparse. The big rigs hadn't begun the haul south from the Canadian Border. Running-water broke the silence.

"Two questions bug me. How did Alan get to the bottom of the cliff and how did Dutch and Will get back to the road and approach the main gate?"

"I've been thinking about that. If they used gliders, where are they? If they ditched on the property, we would have found them. I think that Alan spooked them, and they flew away. That would account for them being at the front gate, "Adam said.

"Suppose they flew back to the village, wouldn't someone have to have brought back to the gate?" Samuel said, glancing in the rearview mirror to see his passengers' reactions.

"Good point. Drive us into the village rather than back to the Monastery," Adam said.

They drove through the village. Nothing there would allow a glider to land, let alone two. When they came to the village's single stoplight, Adam directed Samuel to head south of the town.

"There," Adam said. "Pull in there."

"Just a field. What are we looking for?" Samuel said.

"Tire marks. They'll be about the width of a wheelbarrow tire. Use the spots to light up the area. Stop. Come, Running-water, we walk. Samuel, be on your guard."

The field was heavy with early-morning dew. A local model airplane club used the field. Markers told Adam that. A small building at the end of the field served as a registration booth and snack bar. Fortunately, the club's activities didn't start up until the summer months. They hadn't walked far before they found what they were looking for. Two sets of tire marks; one set overlapped the other. The gliders followed each other in.

Adam and Running-water followed the tracks. Samuel brought up the SUV and lit up the area with its halogen lights. The glider marks ended. Another set of tire marks had left deep cuts in the soft earth, and by their depth, Adam judged a truck had made them. He also found three sets of footprints. The muddy tire tracks indicated the vehicle had turned, left and headed back toward the village.

"No question about it. They flew back here and someone was waiting for them and then drove them back to the Monastery," Adam said.

"Damn. Better call Sheriff Bolton and have a deputy reassigned," Running-water said.

"Don't think that's necessary. Alan was an accident. When one of them clipped him, he staggered and fell over the edge of the cliff. Alan must have spooked them. They didn't land at the Monastery. We'd have seen tire tracks or drag marks if they had. Neither Dutch nor Will smoked cigarettes. Whoever picked them up did; the non-filtered kind and by the looks, hand-rolled. They stood around for a few minutes after getting the gliders loaded."

178

Adam was enjoying the tracking, finding little clues, and putting them together. Weeks in the deep woods with Esaugetuh taught him about animal footprints. The same applied to humans and their vehicles. The freshness of the track is revealed by the amount of earth that had spilled back into the tracks—little dirt meant fresh tracks; a good amount meant old tracks. The tire tracks were relatively fresh. He and Running-water piled back into the SUV. Sam headed back to the village.

"Okay, so who helped them?" Running-water said. "Oh shit. Of course. The two knuckleheads you tried to help. One lives with his mother; the other lives in a shack on one of the outlying roads. When you get into the village slow down Sam. I want to get a fix on the internet."

Within minutes, he had a connection; found the addresses he wanted. They cruised each place. Bud Warren had a truck big enough to carry two folded gliders. He also had a barn.

"Let's go in and get the bastard," Samuel said, surprised by his boldness.

"Can't do that. We'd be charged with home invasion," Running-water said.

"It's nearly daylight. We'll come back later. I can drop in to see how he's doing. Take us home, Samuel," Adam said.

Samuel eased the SUV out of the village and up the long winding road to the Monastery. A few hundred yards from the top Adam ordered Samuel to stop. He got out of the car, walked to a small clearing where a small pond was located. He stood very still; quieter than the early-morning breeze. He sat down, cross-legged and waited.

Running-water followed. As he approached the clearing, he heard Adam's voice. He stopped. Sure, that Adam was praying, he waited, being respectful of such private moments. He quietly walked closer to the pond. He heard Adam talking to someone. He remained in the shadows, watching, unable to believe his eyes. He wiped his eyes, squinted to make sure he was seeing what he saw. He was sure the early-morning shadows were playing tricks. A full-grown male cougar was sitting back on its haunches and looking at Adam.

The cougar quickly shifted its eyes from Adam to Running-water, who had his hand on his gun. Its muscles tightened; the hair on the nape of his neck bristled. Ready to spring into action, it waited. Running-water waited, knowing that an adult cougar could jump thirty feet.

"Sit with us. Come and meet your sacred totem," Adam said as he held up his hand, palm outward, and drew a circle in the air. The cougar relaxed. Running-water was sure he heard the word 'friend.' He sat down, cross-legged, and tried to quiet his breathing. His hands were sweaty. He had pulled one of his Glocks and laid it in his lap as he sat down.

"What the hell are you doing?"

"I am welcoming our friend. Telling him, he is welcome to live here. He is waiting for his mate to return. She is out hunting," Adam said. his voice quietly calm.

180

The large cat's ears perked up. He sniffed the air and growled. His mate answered. He went to the underbrush. A lot of low growling changed into fierce snarls. Everything got quiet.

"Don't move," Adam said to Running-water, who had started to get up.

The mail cougar returned, turned around, and then went back into the brush. More snarling and spitting. A loud crashing of branches filled the air. A female cougar emerged with the male close behind urging her forward. He lay down, looked at Adam, and then licked its paws.

Adam saw the shaft of an arrow sticking out from the hip of the female. Running-water watched in complete fascination as Adam talked to the two animals. He was calming them, assuring them of their safety. Slowly, Adam unfurled his crossed legs and eased himself up to his full height. He moved over to the injured female cat, squatted down in front of her, and held out his hand.

Neither moved. She sniffed his hand and gave it a nudge. Adam ran his finger down the bridge of her nose, gently blew into her eyes. She was under. Running-water had never seen an animal hypnotized. The blue aura engulfed Adam, grew in intensity, and nearly blinded Running-water.

A shrill scream filled the air. Running-water pulled out his hidden gun, blindly aiming it everywhere. He was gulping air. Afraid to fire he shouted, "Damn it all, Adam."

The bright blue light faded. Adam was sitting with both animals. The male was licking his mate's face.

"I had to shove the arrow on through so I could break it. She'll probably have a slight limp, but she's going to be fine. Bring her a handful of water from the pond," Adam said.

Running-water held out his cupped hands to the wounded animal. She took a couple of licks. The male leaned over, put a heavy paw on Running-water's arm, looked at him, and then licked his face. Running-water paled. He heard a voice.

"This is the second time you have come to my aid. I am grateful."

"Good god. No. This is ridiculous. Cougars don't talk. You're playing head games with me, Adam."

"I didn't speak to you. He did. We are old friends. He is the same cougar that stood guard over me in the deep woods above Tahoe; the same cougar that fought the crazed bear, and the same cougar that was in your hospital room when I caught your soul and prevented it from leaving you. You have nothing to fear from these two friends. When we get up to the house, we'll lay out meat for them. I want Samuel to put up no hunting signs all along the property line."

Adam slowly stood up. Shuddered. A chill passed over him. Someone was watching them. Every synapse fired. The hair on his arms stood up, charged by some magnetic force. His ears fine-tuned every sound; his eyes read every movement. He looked, searched.

The hair on the nape of the male cougar bristled; its ears went back, twitched. He hissed as he showed his fangs.

Running-water stood still, gun at the ready. Whatever Adam had felt; he had not felt. Adam signed that they should return to the SUV. Neither spoke until they were inside the Monastery.

"What the hell was going on out there? I don't mind admitting it scared me. I know that there's a spiritual connection between humans and the animal world. You've taught me that," Running-water said. "Got to admit, it was so surreal."

"If we believe in a creator," Adam said, "then it's not illogical that that creator created all things. And if that is true, then all things have an element of the divine creation in them. Some call it the Divine Light. Others call it Deity-in-Posse. Our ancestors appreciated this spiritual continuity that existed in all things."

"So what you're saying is, is you simply responded as one spiritual being to another? Have you always thought this way? Or did it come with your Vision Quest and the search for our father?"

"Inherently, there's always been an underlying sense or feeling that there was something that created. I've always had questions as to what that was. My adopted father never wanted to talk about such things. I drove my philosophy and religious professors crazy with questions. And speaking of questions, while we were with the cougars, did you sense that we were being watched?"

"No. The cats occupied my attention. You think someone is still on the premises?"

"I'm not sure; I've had quick glimpses of shadows and whispered sounds."

"We'll be doubly cautious. You want me to ask Sheriff Bolton to get a warrant for Budd Warren?"

"No. I'll pay him a visit. If I find anything at his place, I'll call you, and then you can see about a warrant. After breakfast, have Samuel bring the limo around front. In the meantime, see if any of the devices used to detect abnormal changes in temperature are usable. If so, set them up. And see if the apparition detecting devices are set back up. I'd like to have the compound monitored."

"You sure you don't want me to go with you rather than Samuel?"

"Yes. He's fine."

Running-water reluctantly accepted Adam's choice. It wasn't that he felt Samuel wasn't reliable; naked suspicion crawled back into his being. Worm-like the suspicion that he was being replaced as Adam's personal guardian wrapped itself around his being. He attempted to rid himself of this ill-begotten feeling by searching for the meters that registered energy presence. Despite busying himself, the nagging suspicion lingered. Biblical Cain and Able ran as a seamless video through his mind as he worked to reconnect one of the devices.

"There's not much difference between Cain and me. I could kill Adam. My God! What am I thinking?"

That thought sent shock waves through him. He raced back into the house and not waiting for the slow creaking elevator, raced up the stairs to the third floor. He pounded on the door, yelling "Esaugetuh."

Daphne opened the door, startled by her brother's wild look. "What is it? Has something happened to Adam?

"No. He and Samuel have gone back into the village. I've got to see Esaugetuh. Where is he?"

"On the deck. I'll get him."

"I'll go out there."

Running-water nearly knocked Daphne over as he rushed past her and out to the deck overlooking the back lawn. He ignored the traditional formality of waiting to be recognized.

"I'm Cain," he blurted.

"What are you talking about?" Esaugetuh said, surprised by the sudden outburst of Running-water.

"Am I like Cain in the Bible? Today, I thought what it would be like if Adam were dead. What it would be like to kill him."

"My God, why?"

"I can't stop the river of suspicions that's drowning me. It's eating my guts. I am sure Adam is replacing me with Samuel and that Adam is really the favored one. I can't stand it any longer. Help me"

"Of course. First, you are just as much my son as is Adam. I love you, just as I love him," Esaugetuh said, reaching out to touch Running-water. "Guess I failed to realize the She-Devil, Moon-Woman, got her hooks into you before Adam used the obsidian amulet of the Wisdom Keeper."

"Can you help me?"

"I'll do what I can, but I think it will take Adam."

"Take Adam to do what?" Daphne asked as she handed them a glass of brandy.

"To get rid of Moon-Woman's curse," Running-water replied.

"Curse? I don't understand," Daphne said.

"I can't explain it right now. Tell Adam I will be at the altar our father built," Running-water said as he got up and left the deck.

CHAPTER TWENTY-THREE

Samuel backed into the driveway so the limo would face out. Bud Warren's place wasn't much more than a lean-to attached to the side of an old barn. Both dilapidated and weather-beaten. A chimney for a wood-burner poked its way up through the roof. Sure that he had seen a feedbag curtain move, Adam waited in the limo. When no one came out, he got out and went to the door. His knock rattled its frame.

"Bud, its Adam. I was in town and thought I'd stop to see how you were doing," Adam said.

The door flew open and Bud Warren hit Adam full force, knocking him to the ground. Cat-like.

Adam rolled over and was on his feet. Bud's kick missed, and he ended up on the ground.

Samuel tried to get out of the limo. In his excitement, he forgot to unfasten his seat belt. "Damn! You'd think I'd learn," he muttered. By the time he was in the open, Adam had raised his right hand, drew a circle in the air. Bud Warren flattened. He struggled to get up from the ground. He couldn't sit up. Adam continued to hold his hand outward, slowly clenched his fist, and then tossed something at the spread-eagled Bud.

Bud Warren screamed; a terrorized man, his scream rose in pitch and then died in his throat—a whimpering gurgle.

Dumbed by this display of Adam's power, Samuel froze in his track, mouth agape. Then he heard Adam say, "Relax, I'm not here to harm you."

187

Adam released his hold. Bud sat up, rolled over, and vomited. He wiped his mouth on his sleeve.

"Are they gone? The worms? They were trying to eat me." He frantically brushed away at his legs. He tried to stand. Adam caught him.

"Guess we'd better get you inside. I'd like to ask you some questions, but I think we should try another healing, first," Adam said, winking at Samuel.

Inside, the one room, and that's all it was—a single room, was strewn with junk; empty pizza cartons, dozens of empty beer cans, and half-smoked cigarettes. Embedded in the walls of the place was the smell of urine and vomit. Adam left the door open and then opened the single window. Dust flew everywhere as he moved the feed sack curtain.

Adam hypnotized Bud in a matter of seconds, instructing him to answer his questions. Bud revealed that the gliders stored in his barn belonged to Dutch and Will; that they had met at the local watering hole, paid him to pick them up at the model airplane landing strip.

"Did you drive them up to the Monastery?" Adam asked.

"Yes."

Do you know how they got the gliders here?"

"They had a fancy rig with one of them enclosed trailers," Bud said.

"If they had a rig, why'd they hire you?"

"Their truck broke down. It's at Jake's in town."

188

Adam released Bud, thanked him for his time, and left, assured now that a third assassin wasn't still on the mountain. On their way up the long drive, Adam had Samuel pull over and stop. He got out of the limo, stood very still, and listened. He waited. The male cougar appeared. Adam followed him to a large hemlock. He pulled aside its long, low hanging branches. Nestled inside was the female. Adam extended his hand, palm up toward the recuperating animal. She sniffed him, licked his hand. Her nose was moist against his hand as she nuzzled him. Carefully, he checked her wound. He passed his hands over the wound. She felt their warmth and began to purr.

"You're doing fine. Good girl. I'll be back tomorrow and check on you again."

Turning to return to the limo, Adam bumped into Esaugetuh.

"We need to talk," Esaugetuh said without first greeting his son

"Man, I didn't hear you approach nor did the cougars indicate your presence. You are something else, Old One. You sure haven't lost your touch. You are distressed. What troubles you?"

"I've sent Samuel on ahead. We'll walk back. That way we'll be private in our talking.

"It seems Moon-Woman got her hooks into your brother. Something we have ignored," Esaugetuh said

"And what about you Old One? What has been her influence on you? Did she get her claws into you as well? Do you suffer, father?

189

"I am not important. Running-water is. He has devoted his life to protecting you and now he says he believes he is Cain from the Christian Bible. He dwells upon killing you."

"I can't believe he'd actually try to kill me."

"He wants you to do a healing. He is at the sacred altar preparing himself. If the She-Devil did leave her mark on him it may take the both of us to deal with it."

As they slowly walked up the mountain Esaugetuh's limp became more obvious. Even though Running-water had done a good job setting it, it has bothered him.

"Where's your cane?" Adam asked.

"I've been trying to get along without it. I have to admit it's much easier coming down the mountain than it is going back up. Mind if we sit a spell?" Esaugetuh said, pointing to a small cement bench.

As soon as they sat down, Adam pushed a button on his cell phone. Within minutes, Samuel arrived on an ATV. Esaugetuh climbed on board and Samuel immediately whisked them away. Adam continued the walk back up the mountain. It gave him time to think about what his father had said. He had a more compelling reason to tarry. Someone had followed him, watched him, and studied him. As he walked along, he was sure a shadow floated low over the grassy area, along the flowerbeds, spread itself out, and disappeared.

"Could have been a low moving cloud casting a shadow, " he thought. He shrugged his shoulders and moved on. He soon was at the central courtyard

190

with its beautiful fountain. It's massive copper and brass eagle with a salmon in its grasp reflected the sunlight. The water bubbled and gurgled over real rocks, splashing down into a large pool. He watched the water; its rhythm soothed him. He synchronized his own rhythm with its ebb and flow. He sat down on its edge, watched the movements of the water.

For a wondrous carefree moment, he transported himself to an earlier time in his life, a time when ugly death was not a companion of his experiences. "How has my life gotten so entangled, so totally maddening, and so awfully cruel? I know I can't protect my young sons from the drama of death, but maybe I can help them understand that it's a natural process. I'm supposed to be a healer, yet so many of those around me are subjected to terrible pain and gnawing fear. No one should have to live in a constant state of fear. I always have more questions than answers. It's always been that way; guess it always will be."

It was her scent that caught him. It brought him back.

"You have a heavy heart, my husband," Daphne said, sitting down beside him. She took his hand, brought it to her lips, and kissed it. She dropped his hand. "Have you been with the dogs? I smell animal on you."

"We have a mated pair of cougars on the premises. The female was shot with an arrow. I removed it. I stopped a while ago to check on her. She's going to be fine."

"Cougars. My god, Adam. Isha and Running-water's twins are out and about."

191

"They will not harm the children or any of us," Adam said. "Come. We must go in now. Running-water needs me." He wrapped his arm around Daphne, gave her an affectionate pat on her behind.

At the steps of the portico, Adam stopped, pulled Daphne to him, and kissed her. He held the kiss, an open demonstration to those who watched that she was his, and they should not trifle with her. Inside, Adam asked Daphne to gather up their children, to get Isha and her twins, and then to join him outside at the altar.

While Daphne and their quadruplets took the elevator down to the second floor to get Isha and her twins, Adam began his preparations for a healing ceremony at the altar built by his father. He showered and then smudged himself with a sage bundle, rubbed oil of lemon, angelica root, and heuchera over his entire body. He felt sensuously alive. Instead of full Indian regalia, he selected a loincloth of deerskin with his totem painted in black and red. He secured the leather tongs on each side and then stepped into a pair of tan leather moccasins. He divided his long hair in half and then quartered that. He created two braids that hung down the front of his broad shirtless chest. In keeping with the old ways, he placed a single eagle's feather into the crown of his hair.

His father had an appreciation for the traditions, and he suspected the Spirits that governed their lives, held tradition in the same regard. He sat down on the floor; legs folded under each other, and clasped his hands together on his lap. He sat still for a few minutes, taking time to regulate his breathing.

Then he began to hum, synchronizing the sound with his body rhythms until a welcome calm bathed him. Once he felt comfortable, he got up and went out onto the balcony, and looked down at the group gathered at the altar.

The sunset's golden-red hues spread themselves over this panorama, adding a singular touch to the landscape. As Adam looked out at this painting, one of the mated eagles flew low along the open area and then shot straight up as it caught a wind current. Its whistle came back loud and clear. It was a good sign. Adam took the elevator to the first floor, went into the kitchen, and exited into the backyard. Esaugetuh was speaking to the assembled group: Brett Montana and Patricia Livingston with her camcorder sat on the ground directly in front of the altar. Behind them was Samuel and Julie, Genevieve Van Batten and Jedediah Woods. Running-water, Isha and their twin boys were on the front right. Behind them were Daphne and the quads. He stayed back, listening to his father.

"For as long as time itself has existed, our world has been a world of one mind—a mind that is both dark and light, creator and created, both part and sum, a totality that is all things unto itself. Sometimes because of a collapse or a rupture, a bent spirit enters our reality, an overly charge emoticon whose only purpose is to alter our reality. Out of ignorance, we call it evil and cry out for mercy. We forget that it has no dominion over us other than that which we give it—by naming it—we bring it into reality. Like the effluent in a sewer, it rushes through our imperfect bodies, drowning us in self-

193

immolation. Because it is both physical and psychological, it is emotion-driven. Because we are interconnected physically, emotionally, and spiritually when one suffers, all suffer; when one is loved, all are loved. My son, Running-water suffers; I suffer, as do all of you. He experiences the pain of self-doubt, the pain of self-negation, and the pain of misguided thoughts. Tonight, I ask you to join me as we draw a circle of love. I ask that you let it reach out to the cosmos to receive nurturing by all that exists there. I ask each to remember that we are a part of the sum and that we are also the total. Each of us here, now, at this moment in time, is connected to that whole. We are inextricably bound to all that has gone on the past, bound by all that is, and by all that can be."

Esaugetuh dug a fire pit. It was made of seven flat stones laid seven inches apart. The scooped-out hollow in the soft earth had at its center a small teepee of sweetgrass laced with a pinch of tobacco. Esaugetuh waved his hand over the teepee and just has it had done when Adam began his vision quest, it burst into flames. Adam joined the group. Running-water stood up, dropping the blanket from around him, revealing his nakedness. He did this so all could see the shame he felt and the terror that ate at his soul. When one is naked, all is exposed. His oiled body reflected the golden-red hues of the setting sun; the light from the small flames in the fire pit bounced off his muscularity as he strode to meet Adam.

"My life is yours, my brother," Running-water said.

194

"And mine yours," Adam said, indicating that Running-water should lie down on top of the altar. "Bring the children and seat them at the head and feet of our brother. Esaugetuh, join me at his side. The rest of you form a circle around us and join hands. Clear your minds of any troubling thoughts; think only of the love in your hearts. With me, call upon the Spirits to free our brother of his pain."

Adam reached across Running-water's body, clasped his father's hands, and began to chant. Esaugetuh's voice joined in. From somewhere off in the far distance the tong-tong drums beat in unison with their chanting. Patricia Livingston felt the vibrations coming up from the earth itself. She felt a life-generating, and inwardly she smiled. The light on her recorder was flashing, an indication that it had been activated; proof that there was sound—the sound of tong-tong drums when no one present had a drum.

Goosebumps scattered along her bare arms. She felt a slight chill as she adjusted her equipment, making sure everything was working. "Maybe I can work this into a documentary," she thought. She zeroed in on the children with her camera. They were radiating a blue aura that vibrated in tune with the chanting of their elders. The blueness, like an early evening mist, grew in size until it arced up from them, spreading out and forming a canopy over Adam, Esaugetuh, and the outstretched naked body of Running-water.

While she made another adjustment on her camera, Patricia glimpsed a movement high up in a tree, directly behind Adam. For an instant, she thought she had caught the last rays of the sun as the evergreen's branches moved in a gentle breeze. "No. That wasn't the sun; wrong direction. Someone wearing glasses or someone with field glasses. Damn. They are at it again. I know someone is watching us. And I'm sure there is more than one. Wonder how they have been able to avoid the high-tech security that surrounds this place. The President of the United States isn't this well guarded. Whew. Talk about Big Brother. He's here. Well, who the hell ever you are I'll find you and when I do you'll wish to God you'd never been peepers. That exactly what you are, peeping toms."

She looked around. Everyone had their eyes closed. None of them would have noticed these interlopers. Her attention shifted back to the blue canopy that enveloped Adam, Esaugetuh, and Running-water. Its translucence fascinated her. She watched it as it flowed, river-like and like the delta of a river, it spread out. She could see the trees and flowering shrubs directly behind Adam. "My God! I'm looking right through him."

She watched, astonished as a vortex formed over the altar. Running-water stretched his arms out from his sides, a Salvador Dali painting if there ever was one. Slowly, he began to float skyward. She moved to get closer, adjusted the camera to a panorama setting. She was looking up into the vortex, refocused her lens. Shapes came into view, faces, distorted with grotesque open mouths and eyeless. They were speeding in every direction, frantic. Spiraling around the outer edges of the vortex, they grew in number. Some dove at

196

Running-water; others seemed to be flying out of him, floating in and out. She heard their high pitched screaming and shuddered. And since they had no eyes, Patricia Livingston knew they were not the watchers.

The vortex spiraled higher and higher into the darkening sky. A bright blue-light, arrow-shaped sliced through the sky, hitting the spinning vortex, and shattering it. Patricia Livingston gasped. An owl hooted, and she heard its wings beating the air as it took flight. "Maybe that's what I saw. No. The hell I did. I know when I'm being watched."

Adam released his grip on his father's hands. Both looked at Running-water laying motionless on the altar. There was no discernible movement of his chest. Adam placed a finger on the carotid artery. Then he opened Running-water's mouth, leaned down, and blew into it. Running-water opened his eyes; looked at Adam and then at his father.

"How fingers do you see?" Adam said, holding up two fingers

"Two. Man, I feel like shit. I thought I was supposed to feel better," Running-water said.

A tug at his hand from his sons brought a smile of recognition to Running-water's drawn face. He gathered them up, hugged them. Isha went to him, kissed him, and whispered in his ear. He blushed as he felt her heat press against him.

Standing up, Running-water embraced his father and then turned to Adam. Tears welled up and spilled down his handsome face.

"I am so ashamed. Can you forgive me? Forgive my pettiness, my jealousy, my ingratitude? Man, I've been such an ass."

Adam grabbed Running-water; gave him a bear hug, lifted him up off from the ground, and swung him around. "There's no shame in being human, my brother. Our harmony was lost because of mistrust and fear. Both caused by suspicion. It separated us; driving us into the darkness of alienation. It was necessary for us to change the negative patterns that had been developing—the base metal of our beings—our egos, which had been denying our Soul Self. It's over and will not be mentioned again."

The assembled group went back into the main house to celebrate. All but one. She had made a promise, and she intended to keep it.

CHAPTER TWENTY FOUR

Patricia Livingston hurried along the walkway to the guest house where she, and Brett lived. She poked around in one of the many unpacked boxes, found what she was looking for. She pulled up a can of mace spray and placed it on her bed. She quickly changed into black sweats and black running shoes. She paused in front of a mirror, checked her hair, and fluffed it out. She realized that she should have her head and face covered. She wanted to make whoever was watching would have trouble spotting her. She went back into their bedroom, pawed around in a closet, found a black scarf. She wrapped it up and around her neck, chin and over the back of her head. Then she pulled it down to cover her forehead. Only her eyes were visible. Mascara. Yes, I need mascara to cover the white under my eyes. Quickly, she applied a generous coat. Looked in the mirror. "Hmm. Not bad. Doubt if Brett could do any better. I should leave him a note."

She went through a checklist; infrared camera, night-vision binoculars, extra disks, batteries, bottled water, couple energy bars, flashlight, first-aid kit, a can of bright pink spray paint, and matches. She couldn't remember why she bought the spray paint. She hesitated as she held the matches. Then she tossed them along with everything else into her black backpack. She turned off the lights, slipped out the door, tested it to make sure she had it locked, and disappeared into the dark.

She stuck close to the shadows of the trees and flowering shrubs as she headed into the thicker wooded area of the compound. It was on the edge of the forested area that she had seen them; had watched them disappear. It was that terrible night Adam fought Moon-Woman. Energized at the prospects of a sensational news story, she staked out a spot she liked, sat down with her back to a tree, pulled out the night-vision binoculars, and began a systematic search of the greenery. The high moon provided just the right amount of light. Slowly, she scanned the lower growth; worked her way up into the taller trees. One tree at a time. Nothing. She reversed the process and then repeated it. Still nothing.

"Maybe I am nuts. It's probably been that owl all along. Easy girl. The first rule of my business is to trust your instincts. Stop doubting." She rubbed her abdomen; she wondered if the old issues were cropping up again. Just nerves. "There was an image on my video—the one that Will Rexford stole. No question about it. Shit! Why haven't I thought of this before? It wasn't his image he wanted to erase; it was their image." image."

Patricia put the binoculars away, picked up her backpack and moved to another area; this time, going deeper into the woods. No paths here. Low hanging branches slapped at her as she pushed her way deeper into the woods. Sometimes she had to crawl on her hands and knees to get through the underbrush. She worked up a good sweat. She stopped, checked her watch. It was an hour since her first stop. Because the going had been slow, she wasn't sure how far she had really gone. She squatted, and then sat all the way down, leaned against a tree, and took a swig of water. She was glad she remembered to bring water. A slight tinge of nausea flooded her stomach. She took another drink of water, swallowing it more slowly.

"They have got to be here. A hundred acres is a lot of ground to cover. They could be anywhere. Maybe I'm all wrong. Maybe they aren't in the deep woods at all; perhaps closer to the house. Maybe like moths, they are attracted to the light. Of course. To firelight. The night of the confrontation with Moon-Woman, Adam built a large fire in the front yard. Yes. That's when I saw them for the first time. I nearly fell out of the tree I was in. Okay, so build a fire," she thought.

Patricia pawed around in her backpack found her flashlight, the one that gave off a blue light. She turned it on, looked around. She found some pine needles and some twigs.

"I need something to dig with. I forgot that in my rush. Oh, hell, just dig with my hands. So, I ruin my nails. They'll grow back."

She began digging with both hands. She dug a small hollow in the soft earth, brushed the dried vegetation away from its edges. She cleared a two-foot space all around her fire pit. She broke some of the branches into smaller pieces and crumbled some pine needles on top. She brushed these into the small hollow she had dug out.

Glad I brought those matches. She struck one, tossed into the fire pit. It didn't light. Damn. She struck a second match and held it to the starter. It

201

burst into flames. She added a few larger twigs, waited for them to catch, and then added a couple of large branches.

She sat up her infrared camera and made sure it was in motion-activated mode. She took out her night-vision binoculars, refocused those, and then placed them by her side. She retrieved one more item from her backpack, the canister of mace. She checked to make sure its nozzle pointed away from her. "I got enough fire stuff to keep it going for at least an hour. Now I wait," she thought.

The warmth of the small fire, the intoxicating smells of the cedars and pines, and the physical exertion conspired against her. Her eyelids grew heavy as sleep conquered her.

And those who watched were pleased with their handy work; gleeful that they outsmarted her again. They would have done more, but the cough of a cougar interrupted their activity.

Brett was the first to find her. She was curled up, next to a tree, sound asleep. The light from his flashlight roused her. She automatically pointed her can of mace in the direction of the light. He whispered to her as he knelt down.

"What were you thinking of? Coming out here alone. Something could have happened to you."

He took her in his arms, pulled her close, kissed her.

"She had a visitor," Adam said.

"Damn! I missed them," Patricia Livingston said.

"Not them. A cougar. Looks like he sat and watched you for quite a while. Grounds still warm. He hasn't been gone long," Adam said.

"We found her. She's okay," Brett said into his Cobra.

"Great. Good news. Samuel and I will head back to the house," Running-water replied.

Patricia, walking arm in arm with her husband, reminded Adam of her earlier video. "Will Rexford stole my video not to erase his photos but to erase our mysterious visitors. Don't you see, Adam? He was working for them."

"So, you're saying these so-called visitors are responsible for all the attempts on Adam and Running-water's lives?" Brett said

"Exactly. Aren't you proud of me?"

"As interesting as your theory is, I don't believe they are responsible," Adam said.

"And why not?" Brett said.

"I do believe Patricia to a point. But whoever they are, I don't believe they are here to harm us. In fact, I believe they are our protectors. If they had meant us harm, they would have done it by now," Adam said.

Adam stopped walking and put his hand to his face. He felt a cool breeze brush against it. "They are with me, watching, and following. Maybe it's no more than protecting us, but I'd like to be sure."

Adam went on into the house; Patricia and Brett returned to the guesthouse. Daylight was approaching, and Adam decided to stay up. He went out on one of the eastern balconies to watch the sunrise. From there he could see the flatlands, the faint glow of light down in the village, and far off, in the distance, he could see the reflected glow on the water that was part of Skagit Bay.

The sunrise was a reminder that there is always a new beginning. He understood what one does with that beginning, determines what other choices can be made.

"My day still holds two vital questions: Who is behind the continued attempts on my life, and who are these Watchers? One thing is for sure; Joseph is dead and Thomas, his brother, is still in a Canadian prison. And I feel Moon-Woman is dead."

He stretched, did some quick bends, and flexed his muscles. He felt them tighten against his shirt.

"What I need is concrete evidence. He smiled as he remembered that Running-water's twins had scanned Christine Lilith Conduit and had transferred the information to his own children. I don't need Christine after all. My children can help me transport, but before I get them involved, I need to make sure there is no danger to them. I'll ask Esaugetuh. But first, the Watchers. It's time to deal with them," he thought.

"I don't know how you can go with so little sleep. It's not healthy," Daphne said, entering the balcony to join Adam. She sat down in a chair next to him.

"Have you ever felt you were being watched?" Adam said.

"Hmm. Now that you mention I do sometimes feel someone is in the house other than those who are supposed to be."

"We have been watched for quite some time. I've sensed them when I've been out on the property. Patricia has seen them. Shadows, mostly. She thinks Will Rexford was trying to erase their images from her videotape. She spent most of the night out there searching the grounds trying to find them."

"Not too smart on her part, I must say. Adam, isn't there such a thing as ectoplasm? I've read something about it. I think it has something to do with the materialization of a spirit. You really think there's more than one?" Daphne said.

"Yes, I do. I've never told you this, but in my past, people who have been involved with Running-water and me have died in strange and unusual ways. For example, when your brother and I were visiting Marie Copa in Arizona, two men died in a parked car just down the street from her apartment. They had been watching us. Then, there were two men in the Pennsylvania jail cell who died in a similar manner. The last two of The Brothers, Philip, and Paul died with similar small holes behind their right ears. Esaugetuh thinks a voodoo weapon from one of the islands was used to kill them. Each of these people tried to kill Running-water and me. And each time it was they who died. For a time I thought Esaugetuh was responsible for their deaths. Now I believe differently."

"Differently?"

"Do you remember seeing a flaming arrow shot in the darkened sky the night, we fought Moon-Woman? I swear I heard someone say, 'There take that, bitch.' I believe it was these watchers."

205

"Do they mean us harm?" Daphne said.

"I don't think so."

"If that's true, then these watchers, as you call them, are capable of killing. And if they are here to protect you, then there must still be danger otherwise they would have moved on."

"Smart girl. I knew there was a reason for marrying you," Adam said, patting her knee.

"There you are. I've b calling you on the intercom. Guess you had it turned off. You need to come and see this," Brett said.

"See what?" Daphne said.

"Patricia's video. We're in the great room."

Adam and Daphne went back into the house and immediately joined the others in the great room. Facing them as they entered was a picture of a cougar on the giant television screen.

"Watch the cat," Patricia Livingston said. "There. Did you see that?" She pushed the back button on her camera and then shot the video forward.

Brett was enjoying the animation of his wife. Her enthusiasm infected the group. "Watch the top of his neck. And listen."

There was no question about it. The hair on the nap of the cougar's neck bristled and there was a distinct low menacing growl.

"Now watch. I'll zoom in. You'll see more that way," Patricia said; her voice resonated with excitement. "I have absolute proof that spirit beings exist. My god, imagine what that means."

It took a minute before the rest of the group focused on the cause of Patricia's excitement.

Slowly, it registered; a slightly different hue to the foliage, which gradually defined itself by blinking. For an instant, its two eyes were visible. Nose and mouth were not visible. On the video, it became agitated and disappeared.

The cougar moved. Then it came back into view again. It sat on its haunches intently listening to something. The video picked up whispering. Patricia turned up the volume. The voices became very clear.

"We cannot dispose of her. She is with child. To do so is a violation of our being."

"But she has seen us. She is a threat to our existence. Certainly, that counts."

"Can't you see she is a special one? The wild beast guards her. We'll have to be direct and reveal ourselves to the one we've been sent to watch and protect, the one that has been called Adam. He will know what to do about the human female."

The group sat stunned. Not believing what they had just heard.

"Good god. Play it again," Genevieve Van Batten said.

"A baby? You're pregnant. You've just blown me away," Brett interrupted. He grabbed Patricia, hugged her, and kissed her.

The video played out, and the screen glowed silver.

"When were you going to tell me?" Brett continued.

"Today. Today I was sure. Now put me down. Well, do I or don't I have the story of a lifetime? No, the story of the century."

207

"Writing about us should be enough; no need to write about them," Adam said.

"Why Adam? My god, how can you not want the world to know?" Patricia said. "I don't get it. You mean you want to deny me my chance at history?"

"This is what I know. These watchers, whoever they are, have the capacity to kill. I also know they have chosen to let you live so that you may give life. Are you sure, you want to take a chance and lose that gift? Of course, I'd like to meet them. I just don't know how."

"That's not fair. My pregnancy has nothing to do with them.

"Do you need to listen to the video again? Good god, Patricia, I can't believe you'd risk our child, our lives together just to get a story," Brett said.

"You're asking a lot of me. I'm a reporter. I have an ethical obligation to reveal this. It's what I do or have you forgotten that?" Patricia said.

"While I was out in the woods, I thought these creatures might be attracted to fire. You know, like moths. That's why I built the fire. I first noticed them when you had built the large fire in preparation for the battle with Moon-Woman," Patricia said.

"I don't think so," Esaugetuh said. "Such a condition would limit them and would limit their activities. No— I think they are invisible by choice. I also believe they take whatever shape and color they wish."

The Watchers watched. That was their destiny. Had those present been observant instead of buried in their own agendas, they would have noticed the subtle changes in the walls surrounding them. The pregnant human female distressed them. And they gave way to their distress by filling the wall with fluid movement; creating rapid ships in color tones. Because another drama was being played out, those assembled didn't catch this fluidity in tone.

Realizing that he would have to be more tactful with his wife, Brett said, "Patricia, you better hang on to your camera. Remember what happened last time." He unplugged the camera and handed it to her.

Because it had been heavily used, its batteries needed recharging but unplugged it was now impossible for her to record the conversation. Her nostrils flared, and her eyes widened. She jammed her hands into the pockets of her sweats, fighting the building anger. "Damn him." He thinks he's so clever." She glared at him.

"What?" Brett said, feigning his innocence.

"That was really bright. And I thought you had some smarts. You knew the batteries were down. How in the hell do you expect me to continue recording with the camera unplugged?"

She blew her pretense of going along. Disgusted, she stomped over to one of the red leather chairs and plopped down. It was then she realized that she had her voice-activated tape recorder in her pocket. "Maybe. Just maybe everything isn't lost after all. It won't be the same as the video but what I have and now with the tape recorder it may be enough."

She fiddled with the recorder, making sure it was in voice-activated mode. No one paid any attention to her squirming in her chair. When Brett came over to her, she looked up at him and whispered, "I love you anyway. I mean it."

It was said more to convince herself rather than her husband.

"Well, Adam what are *we* to do now?" Patricia said.

Perplexed as to what he should do, Adam went to the center of the room and faced the massive fireplace. For some time, he stared at the life-size portrait of his father. Had he but paid attention, he would have seen the subtle movements on the painting. He turned and looked at each of those there, searching each face for an answer. Esaugetuh shook his head. Like his son, he was at a loss.

Adam looked at Running-water's twins and then at his own quads. He felt a tingling, a vibration. There was an oscillating glow about them. He knew indigos were sensitive, more finely tuned to the world around them than others were. The twins were fixated on Esaugetuh's portrait.

"I'd like everyone to sit on the floor; form a semicircle and face me. Daphne and Isha place the children in the center, facing their grandfather's portrait."

One everyone was in position; Adam sat down behind the children. "I've never thanked you for saving my life. Nor have I thanked you for saving my brother, Running-water. For that, I am grateful.

210

I am grateful for your protection. I know you have killed to protect me; to protect us. Because you have, I now offer you the only thing I have, as a gift of that gratitude. However, before I do, I would ask a favor. And I know I don't have such a right. I ask it anyway."

"And what is the nature of this favor?" The voice came from the right side of Esaugetuh's portrait.

Adam noticed the shift in shading; the darker didn't encompass the whole portrait. He sensed there was more than one and looked for another change in color. He gazed at the left side of his father's portrait. He squinted. He saw the understated change.

"Ah. So you have located us." The voices, spoken as one voice, said.

Those seated on the floor witnessed pure energy, radiant beyond their normal imaginations.

"Now then, what is this gift of gratitude you have mentioned?" The voice was not human, nor was it animal. It was more like a robot-generated voice. More like an old tape recorder slowed down. It seemed to come from their whole being.

Gracefully bowing, they floated down from the portrait in a golden light. They seemed particularly enamored with the children: first Running-water and Isha's twins. The twin boys glowed. Then they moved to the quadruplets of Adam and Daphne. They circled around them and appeared to float right through them. The quads glowed.

Adam's words shocked those who sat behind him.

"I offer you my life."

Daphne leaned forward and touched her husband on the shoulder. "And I give you mine."

"Humph. We already have that."

"In that case," Adam said. His voice was cold, deadly cold. "I will spare yours. If you have learned anything about us, you know we'll fight to protect those we love. And if you really have studied us, you'll know our history is filled with those who sacrificed themselves for others and have done so willingly."

"And you call that a value?" The voice on the left hissed.

"Yes. It is; to love others over self," Adam said.

"Nothing like being a hypocrite," the Watcher on the right replied. "Haven't you always preached you have to love yourself?"

"True. If you don't love yourself, you can't truly love others. Love of Self is to recognize self-value—self-worth. If you have none, you have nothing to give. Certainly not love," Adam said.

"And you can love that which you do not know?" said the Watcher on the left.

"We are taught to love the Divine even though we cannot know that which is."

"Nonsense," said the Watcher on the right.

"Who created you?" Adam said.

"A stupid question. We exist," replied the Watcher on the left.

"Who gave you your task of protecting me?" Of protecting us?"

"Upstart. Thinks he knows everything," grumbled the Watcher on the right. "I don't know why we bother."

"You bother because like you, we are an extension of the Divine. And we are because that which exists is in all things, including you. Deny it, and you deny the power that created you."

"We conceded that point."

The seated group sensed unseen movement. Gradually, two forms appeared in front of them. Jell-O-like they slide down the wall and spread over the floor, rising upward slowly changing their shape into something more solid, tunicate-like; yet lacking solidity. Their nearly translucent bodies radiated a lemony glow. It reminded Running-water of Adam when he went into his healing mode. Only his was blue." Hmm. Wonder if there's a connection to these creatures floating in front us. And since Adam and me are twins, why don't I have such powers— abilities as Adam has called them?"

Running-water's thoughts caught the attention of the Watchers.

"There can be only one. You were chosen to be a protector, a role no one else could possibly fill. You have done well, Running-water. You have certain qualities that are essential complements to those of your twin. And like those of the one called Adam, yours will grow. Not just anyone can be designated a protector. You are one of us. There is still much danger. Be on your guard," the right Watcher said.

Running-water turned, looked back at the others, checking to see if they too heard what he had heard. He felt the flush creep into his face.

"That voice was just for you," said the left Watcher, somewhat more raudive than the first. Its liquidity seemed to be swirling, growing brighter and then fading.

"What do you want from us?" Adam said.

"I will tell you, Adam," Patricia Livingston said. "You have my word that I will not go public with my video nor will I reveal your existence. I will destroy the videotape right now."

"And the audiotape in your pocket?" said the left Watcher.

"And that, too," Patricia said, embarrassed that her deception had been caught. "Look, I know you could have killed me anytime you wanted. Why didn't you?"

"We do not kill innocents." Both Watchers spoke in unison.

It took her a moment to understand. Patricia Livingston stood up, reached out to touch what she thought was a face, gently stroked it, and then said, "Thank you. I'd kiss you if I knew where."

"That's not necessary," said the right Watcher; his lemony glow turned slightly pink.

Even though no doors or windows were open, they felt a slight breeze in the room. They were gone. They knew that somewhere—out there—in the light of day or in the darkness of night—they watched. And those on the floor knew they had experienced a rare privilege. After all, how many have seen the Spirit Warriors?

214

The twins yelled, "Look!"

The room filled with the brilliant colors of a rainbow. The everlasting promise.

Patricia Livingston plugged in the camcorder, rewound the video to its beginning. Small beads of perspiration formed along her hairline as she pushed erase. Next, she removed the digital recorder from her pocket and pushed the erase button. She felt sick to her stomach, and it wasn't her pregnancy. Her proof of living spiritual entities gone. She'd feel the pain of that decision for a long time. She shrugged her shoulders. I gave my word, and that's that. Oh, what the hell! I've got something else to occupy me. She rubbed her abdomen.

CHAPTER TWENTY-FIVE

There was a breathless moment for the seated group, an eternity for Patricia Livingston. Adam stood up, went over to Patricia, and hugged her.

"You are truly blessed. Thank you for giving up the very thing your life has been about. You've demonstrated the first of the five principles of Selfhood," Adam said.

"I don't understand. What principles?" Patricia said.

Adam brought out a crystal decanter filled with aged brandy. He served his father first, then Genevieve Van Batten, followed by Jedediah Woods. Tradition mandates respect for one's elders. Severing them first showed respect.

"Returning to your question, Patricia. The first principle of Selfhood is mindfulness. It involves being aware of all existence; not just your own. You just showed that you respect other living things besides yourself. Our friends, The Watchers, have a right to their privacy."

"Respect. What you're talking about is respect," Brett said.

"I'll amen that," Julie said. "I've never felt so loved, so respected, and so welcome in my life. I am certainly one of the lucky ones. No one has treated me with more kindness, respect, and love, as has my Samuel. And tonight I, at last, have a real family," Julie said as she drew an imaginary circle around the group.

"Speaking of family, Isha, your parents must be getting anxious to see their grandsons. Why don't you invite them to come for a visit? And tell them I promise no more shoot-outs. Brett can fly out and pick them up. And while we're at it, Daphne, why not have your mother come out," Adam said. "Brett can pick her up also."

He nodded to Running-water to encourage him to agree. It was a way to remove them from potential danger in New Mexico. Eagerly, Running-water encouraged his wife and sister to accept Adam's offer.

Adam sent Running-water a telepathic message, "Good. Once the families are here, we will take our trip."

"Not without me," Esaugetuh said, joining in the mind-talk

"And don't plan on leaving me out, either," Samuel replied.

CHAPTER TWENTY-SIX

After the arrival of the guests, Adam called Running-water to his office.

"It's time. We need to make our preparations," Adam said.

"What about our father and Samuel?"

"I am concerned that the transfer may be too strenuous for our father. He is old. Samuel is—,"

"Too old?" Esaugetuh interrupted. "Yes, too old for you to be making decisions for me," his voice ricocheted off the walls. "Two sets of eyes are good for searching. Three sets are better."

"Better make that four sets. All you have to do is tell me what to look for," Samuel said as he entered the office. "I said I'd be going with you, and that's that."

Esaugetuh walked into the office. "Amen to that. You plan to combine distance viewing with astral travel?"

"Astral what?" Samuel said.

"It's a form of psychic travel. By using certain sounds to produce specific wave patterns in the brain, we can project ourselves elsewhere," Adam said. "No father, I'm not using distant viewing. I propose sending us into another dimension."

"You plan on going back in time to see at what point Gordon Rapport came under the influence of Moon-Woman?"

"Yes. And then we can work our way forward to determine what he plans," Adam said.

"You know that's very dangerous. Even though the witch is dead there still may be a powerful influence." Esaugetuh said.

"I know Old One. And I am grateful for your concern."

"You'll need to fine-tune Samuel. You and Running-water are already tuned to one another as you are to me. Have you learned the procedure from the scan the twins did of Christine Lilith Conduit?"

"Yes. But I hadn't counted on you and Samuel getting involved. Running-water and I have experienced the mind-meld and have traveled together. If we enjoin Samuel, it leaves weakened security here. Who is to take his place?"

"That's easy. The Watchers," Samuel said.

"What are we to look for?" Running-water said.

"Two things. First, any evidence that would link Gordon to Moon-Woman. And second, if he and the witch are connected, we have to determine to what extent. For example, is he her surrogate? We are to look for evidence, nothing more," Adam said.

"Okay. What do I have to do?" Samuel said.

They sat down in a small circle, legs crossed, with backs erect. They joined hands, one to the other. Adam directed them in meditation. He carefully explained the function of a mantra; that it functions to destroy negative qualities.

"Repeat with me *om namo shivaya.* Keep a steady, unhurried rhythm," Adam said.

Tong-tong drums beat a synchronized rhythm with the chanters. Running-water wondered who was beating them since they were not.

219

"Stay focused," Adam said; his voice maintained the cadence of the mantra.

At the end of fifteen minutes, Adam spoke to each of them, telepathically.

Quiet filled the empty spaces surrounding the four men. Not even their breathing disturbed the air. All time stopped.

The space in their center filled with telesomatic materialization. Gordon Rapport's law office appeared. Samuel gasped. He was unsure of what had happened or how he now found himself in front of a Spanish style brick building. He shook his head, rubbed his eyes with the back of his hand. Blinked. The building was still there. Samuel squinted to read the name on the dirt-streaked window. The lone street light was dim. Yellowed like much of its surroundings. He stepped closer to read the name on the window: Law Offices. Gordon Rapport& Paul Dakota.

"Use the key. Remember? We each have one so whoever got there first could open the office."

Samuel recognized Running-water's voice. He found the key in his shirt pocket. But before he could insert the key in the lock, he was told to stop.

"What?" Samuel said. The sound of his own voice startled him. He yanked his hand and key from the door with such a force the key flew to the ground behind him. "Damn."

"Just bend down and turn slightly to your right. The key is just behind your foot," Adam said.

"There's an alarm system. It's just inside the door on your right. You'll need to punch in a code immediately or the alarm will go off," Running-water said.

You understand?"

Samuel carefully unlocked the door, punched in the code Running-water had given him. A very loud thumping burst of a horn filled the air. Light flooded the office. Samuel felt his heart race. He was sure he was going to pass out. "I'm suffocating. Can't breathe," he thought.

"Easy Sam. Just breathe in and out slowly. Guess Gordon changed the settings for the alarm. Stay put," Running-water said.

"Lock the door. Move away from it. No one can see you. Stay calm. Gordon may arrive. If he does, he may sense your presence. That'll tell us he's under her influence. On the other hand, he may just check to see if anything is missing," Adam said.

"Where are you? Why can't I see you?" Samuel said.

"We're here. I've programmed you so you can't see us. It's a precaution in case Gordon has access to your mind. If he does, he'll think you are alone."

"Watch to see if he opens any hidden areas. If he does, find out how he opens them up," Esaugetuh said. His voice sounded gravelly to Samuel. He was about to ask about it when the door to the office opened.

Two Native police officers, guns drawn, entered. Directly, behind them was an older man. His hair, still in a single braid was thinning and had gray streaks. His appearance surprised Running-water. He aged and badly. His paunch shortened his stature.

221

"Check every room. Make sure no one's in here and then get out," Gordon Rapport said. His wheezing bounced off the walls.

"You better check to see if nothing's missing. You got any cash in the place?"

"No cash. Nothing seems out of place. Check the toilet and supply room."

"Yes, sir. You sure you want us to leave.

"Yes. Fine. Just go."

"Okay. If you need us just hit the alarm."

As soon as the security team was out of the office, Gordon locked the door.

"I know you are in here. Don't try to fool me. Whoever you are, show yourself," Gordon hissed.

Silence.

"I said show yourself. And do it now."

Gordon went to the back of the office. Picked up a can of spray paint and frantically sprayed the air throughout the office.

"What's he doing?" Samuel whispered.

"He thinks the spray will reveal where we are," Adam said.

Rapport began coughing. His breathing labored. He staggered to the door, fumbled with the key to get it unlocked, then flung it open, and sucked in the early-morning air. Once the coughing subsided, he went back inside, and again shut and locked the office door. He looked around. The only prints on the floor were his own. He went to the wall behind his desk, flicked a light switch.

A small door in the wall slid open. A stairway led to a sub-level. Adam and Running-water quickly followed. The dankness was penetrating. And

222

surprising since they were in the desert. They entered a small room, not more than eight by six feet. A single light hung from the ceiling rafter. The only object in the room was an old safe. It was as tall as Gordon Rapport himself; three times his width. Gordon leaned forward to open its door. Adam memorized the combination as Gordon spun the dial. Once the door opened, they could see the safe contained stacks of money.

On the bottom shelf was a black metal box. Gordon reached down and removed the box, shut the heavy door of the safe, and then removed a key from his pocket. He unlocked the box and carefully removed a leather-bound book. Adam recognized the symbol burned into its cover. A serpent crawling out of the ground by a three-branched tree; the same symbol burned into the flesh of several of the murdered Brothers—the symbol of chthonic powers; dark and evil.

Through time, Esaugetuh called out, "He must not be allowed to open that book!"

"Understood," Adam said.

Gordon Rapport checked the safe, spun its dial, and started back up the narrow stairs. The light went out. He stopped his climb. He felt very warm. His heart pounded in his ears. " I can't breathe. I got to get air." Slowly, he inched his way to the top. "I swear I left the door open. I should see the light from the office. Someone's here."

His cream died in his throat. He fell backwards, tumbled down the stairs.

"I'll go down there and see what happened. Strange that the door should have closed like that," Adam said.

"Do not go down there."

"What? Running-water was that you?"

"No."

"Sam? Did you speak to me? Adam said.

"No. What was that awful scream?"

The telesomatic materialization that had appeared in their center disappeared. They slowly unfolded their legs, stretched, and then stood up. Esaugetuh was the first to speak.

"We have powerful friends."

"The Watchers?" Samuel said.

"I suspect we've seen the last of them. They've completed their assignment and so have we. It's over," Esaugetuh said.

"You're not saying anything, Adam. Something still bothering you?" Running-water said.

"We don't know what went on in that hole in the ground. I won't celebrate our freedom from the constant threats until I know. Maybe the scream wasn't a scream of death, but maybe, just maybe it was one of transformation."

"Transformation?" Samuel said.

"Yes. Into something more hideous. Only time will tell."

THE END

Also by Norman W Wilson, Ph.D.

Textbooks

How to Analyze the Short Story with Arthur W.
Savage
The Humanities: Contemporary Images
Butterflies and All That Jazz with Drs. James G.
Massey and Arthur J. Powell
Windows and Images: An Introduction to the
Humanities with Drs. James G. Massey and Arthur J.
Powell
How to Make Moral and Ethical Decisions A Guide

Novels
The Shaman's Quest
The Shaman's Transformation
The Shaman's War
The Shaman's Genesis
The Making of A Shaman

NONFICTION
Shamanism What It's All About
DUH! The American Educational Disaster
So You THINK You Want to be A Buddhist?
Promethean Necessity & Its Implications for
Humanity
Activating Your Spirit Guides
Shamanic Manifesting
The Shaman's Journey through Poetry with Gavriel
Navarro.
Healing The Shaman's Way
How to GET What You Really WANT
Reiki The Instructors' Manual
The Sayings of Esaugetuh

www.ingramcontent.com/pod-product-compliance
Lightning Source LLC
Chambersburg PA
CBHW051822090426
42736CB00011B/1608